P9-CRI-220
With my
thanks!
Beryl

LEAVING SOUTH DAKOTA

A Memoir of a Jewish Feminist Academic

Beryl A. Radin

www.mascotbooks.com

Leaving South Dakota: A Memoir of a Jewish Feminist Academic

The author has tried to recreate events, locales, and conversations from her memories of them. In some instances, names and details of some individuals, such as physical properties, occupations, and places of residence, may have been changed.

For more information, please contact:
Mascot Books
560 Herndon Parkway #120
Herndon, VA 20170
info@mascotbooks.com

Library of Congress Control Number: 2016920268

CPSIA Code: PBANG0117A
ISBN-13: 978-1-68401-108-7

Printed in the United States

"The Jews' greatest contribution to history is dissatisfaction! We're a nation born to be discontented. Whatever exists we believe can be changed for the better."

Shimon Peres

PRAISE FOR
Leaving South Dakota

"A Jewish feminist from South Dakota whose political travails span the civil rights and labor movements? Radin weaves an engaging, moving, and hilarious story of how the values and lessons from her formative years lead her to participate in political struggles for social change, to take a Ph.D. at Berkeley in Social Policies Planning, to serve as a special advisor in the U.S. Department of Health and Human Services during the Clinton Administration, and to become an award winning academic, teaching and conducting research around the world. This is a beautiful and powerful memoir of an extraordinarily wise academic and practitioner whose life has spanned over seven decades. This book will make you laugh out loud."

Norma Riccucci,
Professor, Rutgers University

"Beryl Radin has written an affecting memoir of her life and career. As a fellow South Dakotan, I have lived parts of her story myself and know where she began and how she has flourished from that base. She is a wonderful writer and a friend to every reader. And she provides a compelling history of how and why she continues to make a difference for all of us."

Paul Light,
Professor, Wagner School of Public Service,
New York University

"There are few people who live extra-ordinary lives – moving ahead of their times, and Beryl Radin is one such pioneer. Her memoir is a tribute to the richness of having open minds and embracing cultures and diversity in their truest form – yet remaining fundamental to your core value-systems and moral codes, which in India we call "Sanaskara." Beryl Radin's unrelenting commitment to civil rights and feminism – so well charted out in this memoir – and brilliant contribution to policy have remained a deep influence on moving my compass towards progress of women: our 'soul sisters!'"

Poonam Barua,
Founder Chairman, Forum for Women
in Leadership, WILL Forum India

"From childhood in the Jewish community of Aberdeen, South Dakota, to a career as a professor of public administration at major universities, this luminous memoir details a woman's path through family challenges, a liberal arts education, professional training, and a life of research and teaching. It is a distinctly American story of the opportunities afforded thoughtful women to succeed through talent and grit in the second half of the twentieth century. Radin's lively account of her struggles and successes and her travels and travails will resonate with others who have espoused progressive causes over the past five decades. It is also an important feminist document of one woman's fashioning of a meaningful life in a time of rapid social change."

Judith R. Baskin,
Philip H. Knight Professor of Humanities,
University of Oregon

"Beryl Radin's memoir takes the reader into little known history. Her descriptions of growing up as a Jew in 1930s-50s small town South Dakota reveal a unique part of ethnic life. Her feminist stands in the 'Second Wave' of American women's rights are seen as part of her activities in the wider civil rights movements of the 1960s and 70s. This is a book which expands our understanding of the late twentieth century."

Marjorie Wall Bingham,
Author of *Women in World Cultures*

"Beryl's fascinating and entertaining memoir offers wonderful insights on her highly productive and important career as an academic from small town South Dakota. Her very insightful book provides many interesting reflections on her professional and personal choices that were shaped by her family, education, and Jewish faith as well as feminism and the Civil Rights Movement. Her book is a vivid portrait of her own life's journey and the dramatic policy and cultural changes in America in the last several decades."

Steven Rathgeb Smith,
Executive Director, American Political Science Association

ACKNOWLEDGEMENTS

I want to thank a number of family members and friends who were invaluable participants in this writing journey. My brother Arthur and my cousin Daniel Edelman lived through much of this story and tested my memory. And I also was assisted by advice from friends, including Gene Bardach, Judith Baskin, Bobbie Bellman, Marjorie Bingham, David Cohen, JoAnne Earp, Aviva Futorian, Megan Helzner, Jeff Mayer, Alice Medrich, Karen Nelson, Deborah Premsler, and Nancy Schlossberg.

TABLE OF CONTENTS

AN INTRODUCTION:
Writing a Memoir

I've always had a difficult time responding to the question: "where are you from?" I don't always know what the questioner means by that query. Is it a way of seeking information about the respondent's class, family relationships, religion, or community without dealing with the detail of these topics and thus avoiding controversy? Does it automatically ask for a geographic location where they spent their growing-up years?

Granted, most people answer that question with a geographic location. But that has seemed inappropriate and inadequate to me. When I answer that question literally and tell the questioner that I am from South Dakota, it usually evokes a blank stare that stops the conversation from developing. I really have never figured out why this happens. Is it because the questioner has no idea what it means to be from South Dakota? It is almost always beyond their personal experience. Indeed, when I went to college and gave my friends my standard answer to that question, one of my acquaintances decided that I had created an answer as a way of avoiding my reality – that I was really from Brooklyn. An outspoken Jewish woman with strong political views couldn't be from South Dakota. And, thus, my friend never believed me.

It is hard to know what constitutes the process and experience of writing a memoir. The story that I have tried to tell in these pages spans eighty years. But it is not only the years that have elapsed that frame this story but also the acknowledgement that my life never took a predictable pathway. Probably growing up as a first generation American in a small South Dakota city tells an important part of that story. If I had grown up in New York City, Chicago, or Philadelphia I could describe some patterns that others might find recognizable. It would have been likely that I would have lived in a largely Jewish neighborhood in a city, surrounded by multiple generations of family members.

But that was not my experience. I grew up in a city of 20,000 residents, part of a very small Jewish community that was composed of less than twenty families. And it was not the experience of my parents, both of whom came to the U.S. in the early years of the 20th century, grew up in the Midwest, and chose to marry and start a family in Aberdeen, South Dakota. They found a way to become a part of that society.

But at the same time that my parents chose a very atypical life for immigrants of their era, they also structured their day to day life in ways that illustrated the culture of Eastern European Jews. They were both a part of the American experience but also continued the values of generations of their ancestors. They lived through the economic travails of the American depression, tried to make some sense of the impact of the Holocaust and World War II, and remained committed to both the values and traditions of Judaism. It seemed to me that my household was unlike that of most people in the South Dakota community in terms of the availability of books, music and art. I seemed to know that there was another world outside of my hometown and my house that touched both economic and political realities of the American society. While I seem to have had very different ways of organizing my expectations about the future, I could not describe them to either myself or to others. My earliest memories are a combination of living in multiple worlds.

I became comfortable telling people that I knew from the age of four that I would not spend the rest of my life in Aberdeen. It was my way of saying that I had no idea of how my life would turn out. I had no idea where I might live or what either my personal or career path would be. Not only did I fail to follow a predetermined or defined pathway, I really didn't know the likely outcome of most of my decisions.

Those early experiences probably gave me a sense of experimenting with ways to fit into an unknown society that – on its face – did not seem comfortable to me. The story I tell in these pages describe experiences that were based in many different locations, both in the US and around the globe. I also did not know what my professional identity might be. I explored many different jobs and experiences until I eventually found a way to find an answer to the question, "What do you do?"

This is not the way that memoirs are usually constructed. Most memoirs are written by individuals whose names are known to potential readers. These readers are interested in details about the writer's background, how that individual developed, and their memories and accounts of their lives.

This memoir is somewhat different. The main subject of this memoir is not the detail of my life. Instead, its focus is the world in which I have lived. It begins in the late 1930s and continues through the first decades of the 21st century. This was a period of immense change in the US. I have attempted to provide a picture of a constantly changing environment. Unlike most memoirs, that picture becomes the foreground – not the background – to this story.

Of course that picture is presented through my accounts of my personal experience with that change. Like others of my age, I have experienced incredible shifts in the society in which we have lived. My life unfolded in ways that I could never have imagined because of the creation of new opportunities – as well as new problems – involving economic, political, and social changes. In many ways, I was a passenger on a journey of change.

WRITING A MEMOIR

When I found myself in the last years of my seventies, it became obvious to me that I had not really reflected on those seven plus decades. It wasn't that I avoided self-reflection. Rather it was that I saw my years as a series of episodes that did not seem to be drawn together in a coherent whole. While each of these episodes could be described in some detail, they did not provide a clue about the threads that held them together. My life choices did not fit into any clear pattern. I often thought that I was born out of "sync" and had more in common with the youth of the

21st century than my chronological contemporaries. Yet I continued to do some things that did not fit any known pattern and cobbled together bits and pieces of different interests, expectations, and behaviors.

My career development illustrated that dilemma. I could not plot the pathway of jobs and experiences along a single line. It was rare for me to anticipate the next steps I would take in my professional life. Yet the result of a series of jobs over half of a century generated some recognition of achievement.

I tried at least once before to sit down to write a memoir because it seemed to me that my life has paralleled a period that could be of some interest to my family and those whose lives have intersected my own. But that attempt read more like an academic account of experiences and events. It did not provide a reader much of a picture of a person who tried to find coherence in a world of change, living with often conflicting demands that emerged from past experiences.

It was my fairly recent discovery of a box of letters from and to my parents in their pre-marital year and early years of marriage that opened my eyes to some of the patterns that emerged from their relationship. There were many surprises in that box but the major disclosures dealt with my mother. I found that my image of her was – at the best – limited and – at the worst – very misleading. I realized that my parents – and I – had constructed a life that seemed always to be made up of attributes from multiple worlds. We were constantly balancing these diverse attributes and rarely appeared to be engaged in a clear path that was predictable. Whether we call these attributes conflicts or contradictions, I learned to find a way to live with a foot in separate settings.

It was clear that I was continuing a pattern that was created by my parents and by their families. At first I thought that I was experiencing what others have called marginality – a pattern of operating at the boundary of a system or culture. But that term often has a negative context and is used to denote insignificant or minor behaviors. I like to believe that my pattern is more positive and that it provides a description of a pattern of balancing multiple perspectives. If I thought of this as a theatrical production, I seemed always to be trying to play several roles at the same time.

The pages that follow depict a ride through these worlds. It moves through the world of the immigrant family to their Americanization, dealing with the depression, family tensions, and tragedies. It is located in a small city in South Dakota but at the same time moves across the country and around the globe. It is rooted in Jewish traditions but reaches toward decades of social and political change within the United States and beyond.

Among the issues that illustrate this story are the experiences of a first generation American growing up in South Dakota; the experience of Judaism, the synagogue and the creation of Israel; family traits and practices (including cooking); dealing with politics and social change (including the labor movement, the civil rights movement, and the women's movement); discovering the bureaucracy; crafting an academic career; and discovering globalization.

My memories of the experience moving through these years are filtered through the impatience of a child (and subsequently a woman) who never learned to color inside the lines of the coloring book, wouldn't take an afternoon nap, and sometimes failed to follow the directions spelled out in a recipe. This impatience and sometimes sloppiness took me in multiple directions. Some were self-indulgent but most were usually interesting. These experiences often allowed me to devise somewhat unlikely ways of putting the pieces together.

The threads that link the chapters that follow illustrate this pattern. Each of the areas that are discussed show how families and individuals are not easily assigned to a single category or classification. My parents were immigrants but also proud Americans. My mother and father were concerned about their families but also willing to adventure into new settings. I am a first generation American but also someone who finds meaning in the traditions and identities of earlier generations. I am a child of the Midwest but couldn't wait to explore the rest of the world. My efforts at crafting a career always seemed to be balancing divergent approaches: analyzing the world but operating as an advocate within it. Similarly, I seem always to find ways to link theory and practice. I focused on the U.S. policy world but was always looking for lessons from other systems. The major theme of the book presents my life as one of constantly balancing multiple interests that have emerged through a period of great change in the U.S.

TELEVISION WATCHING AND MULTIPLE EXPECTATIONS

I have tried to illustrate this combination of multiple expectations by describing my television watching patterns. All but a few of my closest friends have no idea that I am a television junky. They would be shocked to learn that the minute I come into my house or enter a hotel room I turn on the television set. My friends might expect me to switch on CNN, MSNBC, or even Al Jazeera America. Or perhaps turn to *Masterpiece Theatre* on my three public television channels. But they wouldn't expect me to watch *Keeping Up with the Kardashians* or *Fashion Police*, let alone *NCIS* or *Bones*. And if I am out of the U.S., I turn on the TV whether or not I understand the language being spoken.

I am an enthusiast of an eclectic array of programs that doesn't fit the image of a nearly retired academic with a publication record of a dozen books and many articles. If I had been a participant in the Nielson rating system of television watching, I think that it may have been hard for those pollsters to categorize me and my viewing pattern.

How did I become this person? Is this an escape from the university and the stereotype view of a professor? But I wasn't always a professor. Where did this pattern come from? Is it a way of tuning out the world or tuning it in? Is it my way of reaching out to a world that is far from my personal experience? My behavior suggests that it is difficult to categorize an individual through clear and simple categories, such as High brow or Low brow (as Russell Lynes suggested).

My television watching pattern probably had its roots in the way that I used the radio in my early years. I would return from elementary school in the late afternoon and usually switch on soap operas. I don't have a clear memory of why I was intrigued by those programs; they were clearly situated in a world very unlike mine in South Dakota. And later, when I would sit down to do my homework in junior high school and high school, I always had the radio on. The radio was my colleague and I didn't distinguish between the music that emerged from that little box and other types of programming. In later years, I learned that many women pointed to a similar behavior as a way of learning about multi-tasking. For me, it was also a way of transporting me away from my day to day life to other possibilities and other places.

I was already in college when my family finally purchased a television set (it took a while for a small city in South Dakota to have television available). I spent one summer glued to the television set watching the Army McCarthy hearings. Given my interest in politics, that was a likely choice. But when I had visited relatives in Minneapolis some years earlier (they had television available much earlier), there was a clue that I was willing to watch anything that appeared on that small black and white screen. I can still see those fuzzy images of the puppet Howdy Doody on the screen. I really was too old to watch that children's program but was lured by the potential of that little box.

Recently I discovered that television dependence has received attention from the American Psychiatric Association. While not recognized as a mental disorder, it has been described as similar to pathological gambling. Perhaps my television watching pattern is a form of addiction. But I like to think that it stems from something else. I don't want to be labeled or categorized in a single, stereotypical fashion. I have almost always been seeking ways to combine multiple traits. And actually being a television junky provides me with images and vicarious experiences that allow me to visualize others' worlds and responses to changes in a shared environment.

Usually my behavior around these patterns is private and doesn't reach the attention of others. Their image of me is often defined by stereotypes that emerge from my professional role. Some years ago, I was working at the Office of Management and Budget in the New Executive Office Building in Washington, D.C. My office was next door to a colleague (a political appointee) who had a poster on his wall of actress Farrah Fawcett dressed in a wet swimming suit. I was annoyed at that sexist picture and had an opportunity to retaliate when I hung a poster in my office of John Travolta dancing in *Saturday Night Fever* that a friend had sent me. When my colleague saw that poster, he was clearly disturbed but didn't connect his poster to mine. He spent the rest of the day walking around the office muttering, "Did you see that poster in Beryl's office? And that woman is a professor!"

THE ORGANIZATION OF THIS MEMOIR

This memoir is organized in three sections. The first section introduces my family (both the extended family and my immediate family), growing up in South Dakota as a Jew, and learning that my view of my mother turned out to be very inaccurate. It is titled A Jew in South Dakota. The second section is entitled Leaving Home. It discusses my experience chronologically related to a number of themes that focus on my education, travel, women's issues, Israel, and a few other topics. And the third section is entitled Crafting a Career and discusses my path to experimenting with and eventually finding an appropriate career.

There are three themes that emerge from these pages. These themes are not unique to me, although they may have been played out in somewhat unusual settings. As you read the pages that follow, you might think about the following:

Theme One shows that people change but usually maintain attributes of their earlier life. My story begins in Aberdeen, South Dakota, and draws on those experiences that are rooted in my family, the community, and in Judaism.

Theme Two indicates that few of us can be described clearly but rather contain contradictions and conflicts as we move through the world. My story illustrates several of those contradictions. They include the conflict between change and tradition (especially dealing with Judaism), operating inside or outside the "system", drawing on skills as an analyst or as an advocate, and working as a practitioner or an academic.

Theme Three acknowledges that change comes in unexpected ways often as a result of unanticipated experiences. Most of us live in the midst of a fairly chaotic world and try to be open to new possibilities that may change the direction of earlier plans.

PART I
A Jew in South Dakota

CHAPTER I
The Box

I'm not sure why I dug out some boxes that hadn't been opened since my last move a decade ago. Evidently I was looking for something but I can't remember what it was. Buried in a closet was a small box (one that had originally contained soap) that didn't look familiar to me but I opened it. It didn't contain whatever I was searching for but I was mesmerized by its contents. Neatly stacked in the container were yellowed letters, most of them still in their envelopes that dated from the early 1930s. Most of the letters were a part of an exchange between my mother and father. This type of exchange seemed far from that devised in the 21th century's world of text messages and cryptic comments. But the box also contained examples of my mother's schoolwork and a copy of her high school graduation program from 1918. Interspersed in the contents were photographs of my parents and their families.

That first glimpse of the contents brought forward an incredible flood of memories of my parents. I thought that I had a fairly good sense of those individuals – the memories I thought were sharp in reality were very limited. That wasn't surprising since my father had died when I was ten years old and my mother died more than forty years ago. But my perceptions of these individuals turned out to be quite misleading.

Most of the letters in the box were exchanges between my mother and my father less than a year before they were married and even before they were engaged. The exchanges were almost like a conversation between the two and it was easy to see the movement from their enthusiasm of meeting each other to a relationship of intimacy. The letters continued through the engagement, planning for their wedding, and then their early years of marriage and my birth.

The stories that had been told to me over the years had given me some idea about that period but it certainly didn't capture either the personal or professional experiences of my parents during those years. When I tried to combine the family tales with what I could glean from the letters, I discovered two individuals whom I had not known and whom I found intriguing. In effect, I was meeting two new people. I had known that both of them were immigrants to the U.S., coming from the area that is now Belarus early in the 20th century – the period where many Jews from Eastern Europe arrived in the U.S. But I didn't know much more than that.

THE FAMILIES

My mother came to St. Paul in 1904 with her family when she was about four years old and thus spent most of her life in the U.S. My father came later, around 1908 when he was approximately twelve years old, arriving in Milwaukee with his family. Unlike many immigrants of the period, both families did not stop in New York but went straight on to the Midwest. Both grandfathers had jobs that were arranged before they left Europe. My maternal grandfather was hired by the St. Paul Jewish community to run their Talmud Torah – the center for Jewish education. My paternal grandfather had been hired by the Milwaukee Jewish community as the shochet, the individual who oversees ritual butchering to assure that the meat was Kosher.

For many Jewish immigrants of that period, leaving for the U.S. was a result of various forms of anti-Semitism, particularly pogroms (violent riots aimed at massacre or persecution of Jews) or conscription of young men into the army. Both of my families had different reasons for their arrival. My mother's family came to the U.S. because my grandfather was the younger son of a rabbi. His older brother inherited the rabbinate from his father and so my grandfather had to find an alternative job that seemed to draw on his rabbinical training. Along came the Talmud

Torah in St. Paul. Ironically, that difficult decision to come to the U.S. allowed him to survive the Holocaust. An oral history done by the Institute for Jewish Research (known as YIVO) from a resident of the town where the family lived described the Nazi's taking away my great-uncle the rabbi along with the man who was the president of the congregation. When I read that, the Holocaust became very real.

My father's family had a different reason for leaving. My paternal grandfather had owned a mill outside of the shtetl (the Jewish community) and was fairly prosperous doing business with non-Jews in the community. However, there was no medical treatment available in that area and after several deaths in the family a decision was made to leave the area and find a livelihood in the U.S. where medical care would be available. Somehow the Kosher butcher shop in Milwaukee materialized. It was a job that had status in the Jewish community although was not a religious position.

While the two families had somewhat similar experiences coming to the U.S., they were quite different from one another in other respects. My mother's family was from a long line of rabbis both on her father's side and even more importantly on her mother's side. My grandmother's father was a well-known rabbi in a town called Romanova in the same general region as my grandfather's parents. Both sets of rabbis appeared to have been associated with the group called "mitnagdim," the branch of Judaism in the Minsk-Pinsk area at the end of the 19th and beginning of the 20th century that concentrated on highly intellectual Talmud study and represented the opposition to more emotional Hasidism. From the discussion in the family, my father's family seemed to have been more involved with the non-Jewish community as merchants and my father remembered hearing his father speak both Russian and Polish as well as Yiddish. While observant, the men in this part of the family were not educated in yeshivot, the traditional educational setting.

MY PARENTS

My mother: I'll start with my mother, Sophie. She was the eldest child in the Edelman family of six children – three boys and three girls.

The first two children came to the U.S. as immigrants while the four remaining siblings were born in the U.S., in St. Paul, Minnesota. I hadn't realized it before reading the box of letters but she seemed to have had the classic characteristics of the eldest child. She saw herself as a responsible person, both inside the family and in school. As I learned from reading the letters, she moved beyond traditional expectations of a woman in the family. But the family carried on some of the traditional behaviors they brought from Europe. My grandfather focused on his teaching and learning and seemed to be quite unaware of the dynamics of living in the U.S. My grandmother was the link to the outside world and my mother would tell me stories about going to work in a laundry with her mother when she was very young to earn extra money for the family. While this was a traditional behavior in the shtetl, my grandmother seemed to resent it. Evidently it was one thing to play that role when your husband had status in the community but another when the new culture didn't value his learning. Yet my grandmother was quite entrepreneurial. As a child I was regaled with tales about my grandmother making wine during prohibition and selling it to the firemen in the fire station across the street from their house. I was quite intrigued by the story as a child, given the illegality involved in the operation.

I had the sense that my grandmother felt that she had married below her appropriate status. Her family seemed to have been a part of an intellectual elite and she felt that her arranged marriage (even though it was to a son of another rabbi) did not meet her expectations. Evidently her sisters had married rabbis, not teachers of young children. The house that she organized in the U.S. was full of interesting photographs (including a large photograph of her father glaring down on the dining room table), an old-fashioned icebox, and furniture that was sometimes uncomfortable and scratchy. The round oak table in the dining room was clearly the center of the house. But my grandparent's house in St. Paul had a swing on the front porch that lured the grandchildren outside of the house to avoid its unfamiliar smells and the tension found behind its doors. This was not a happy family and it was clear to me – even as a child – that problems existed within the house. The two youngest siblings seem to have absorbed the tension to a point of experiencing serious mental health issues.

I always thought that my mother identified more with her father than with her mother. To me her father was a gentle person who cared about teaching and producing beautiful Hebrew calligraphy with gold and silver trimming. The Talmud Torah was really the centerpiece of his life and when he was forced to retire, his energy evaporated and he quickly declined. I couldn't really communicate with him since he spoke very little English. By contrast, my grandmother always seemed to be yelling at him and at her children. She was a tough lady who liked to talk about politics and her English was understandable. I thought it was strange that my mother – a grown woman – was still the object of criticism from her mother. But since the exchange between the two of them was always in Yiddish, the guttural sounds of that language probably misled me to overemphasize the anger that was being expressed.

Until I read the contents of the box, I had a picture of my mother that fit many of the traditional stereotypes about a woman of that era. While she was the eldest child in the family, I believed that her two brothers (next in line) received more attention from their parents, particularly from their mother. I thought that my mother was compliant, someone who didn't rock the boat, and did what was expected of her. Sometimes I actually thought of her as a wimp.

I wasn't surprised, however, that one of the documents in the box was the program from my mother's high school graduation. She was listed in three places – as someone on the honor roll; as someone who had completed the teachers' course in the class of 1918 at Humboldt High School; and as the person who read her essay to the assembled group on "A Lesson in Modeling." She did not appear on the list of those who completed the college preparatory course (although based on the names in the listing, a number of Jewish students had completed that curriculum).

I realized that the title of the essay had a double meaning. My mother rarely told me much about her childhood but she did tell me that she became very interested in sculpture when in high school. This interest upset her father based on the traditional Jewish argument drawn from the second of the Ten Commandments that "you should not make for yourself a sculptured image, or any likeness of what is in the heavens above or on the earth below, or in the waters under the earth." Evidently that led to an episode in which her father destroyed the piece she was working on. Somehow, however, she salvaged a piece of her work, a child's head that lives on my bookshelf today. I had a lot of difficulty assimilating that story about my grandfather's action. The gentle, little man who didn't seem to have a mean bone in his body had done something that I couldn't absorb. It would have been fascinating to find out what my mother's graduation essay argued.

I do not know what my mother did immediately after graduating from high school. I know that despite her academic achievements she did not have the opportunity to go on to higher education. Her second brother did go to the university later as did her youngest sister. But several years later my mother made a dramatic shift in her life. Somehow she convinced her parents to allow her to go to New York City. A close cousin of her mother's (married to a rabbi) lived across the Hudson in New Jersey and evidently that household was viewed as a safe place for her to use as a family base.

As a child I did learn that my mother had lived in New York City for about ten years; it was difficult for me to absorb that information. Because I had a picture of her as a compliant and shy personality, I was convinced that it was a miracle that she didn't get lost in the city or confused about the complexity of the subway system. I still don't know whether my lack of information about that New York City decade resulted from my disinterest in her earlier life or whether she was reluctant to share that part of her experience with me. I did know that she lived in a residential hotel for women in Manhattan (not the famous Barbizon but something akin to that) and that she worked for an Oriental rug importing company during most of the period. The rugs that she obtained as a result of that job were an important part of my growing-up and I actually became a rug collector as an adult.

Going through the contents of the box forced me to explore the possibility that I was, indeed, my mother's daughter. Thinking about her life in New York City made me realize that her search for independence from her family seemed very familiar to me.

The few photos that I saw from that period reflected her interest in fashion and her stylish attire. At one point I learned that she had taken elocution lessons to rid herself of her Midwestern accent. The photos depicted her as a lively person with a number of friends. There were bits and pieces of other information sources. I remember that someone told me that she left New York City because she had an unhappy romance there and sought refuge back in St. Paul but I never learned much more about that and didn't ask her about it.

While this information about New York City was intriguing, I wasn't able to integrate it into my existing image of my mother until I opened the box of letters and photos. There were two types of letters that gave me some sense of her life in New York. One set of letters came from her Oriental rug business employers. She was working for a firm that imported rugs and also manufactured rugs with branch offices in more than ten U.S. cities and a Fifth Avenue headquarters. She evidently had a health scare in 1930 and went back to St. Paul to recuperate. The letters from her employers indicated that she was an essential part of the staff; her role was more than clerical and her employers were concerned about her absence. One wrote, "I shall miss the Secretary who was with my Department at the beginning, and was always so keen about the work, and bright even at the nastiest moments of pressure."

She returned to New York and to the Oriental rug business by early 1931. One of her employers was on a business trip to Minneapolis where he was visited by my mother's brother. In a note to my mother, the employer wrote, "I think your people quite accept the fact that you want to work in New York. Your brother said St. Paul's didn't keep you interested enough." But by 1933, she returned again to St. Paul and notified her employers "that this time it would be best for me to remain at home." The reasons for this return are not clear but they appear to coincide in time with the meeting between my mother and father in Minneapolis.

It was during this period when she returned to St. Paul that my mother received a number of letters from her New York friends. Those letters describe a life that was quite different than what I had imagined. First of all, my mother had decided not to use her given first name of "Sophie" when she arrived in New York. Instead, she used her middle name, "Mattalie," (a bit more exotic) and her friends seem to have adopted that in their communications with her. Their concerns seemed to be those of classic New Yorkers. They wrote about cultural events, books they were reading, and shopping expeditions. And like many young New Yorkers, they were changing their housing arrangements quite frequently. Their correspondence often focused on healthy food and they exchanged tips for assuring that they were in good health.

The comments in the letters seemed far away from the conversations that could have been expected to emerge from a traditional observant Jewish household. Those kinds of conversations may have taken place when she visited her relatives in New Jersey but they were not the exchanges between friends. In addition, these women were all employed, often in settings where they felt that their skills and abilities were not appreciated. I did not expect to read classic feminist concerns from these pages and thus was surprised. It had been my impression that the feminism of the 1920s and 1930s came not from women with immigrant backgrounds but from those from more elite backgrounds. And I clearly had not anticipated that my mother's decade in New York City represented her search for independence and cosmopolitan experiences.

Her return to St. Paul continues to be somewhat of a mystery to me. Was it because of some problems in the family? Did she feel a sense of responsibility for either her parents or her younger siblings? Did the economic problems created by the depression play any role? Was she escaping from some unpleasant personal situation in New York? Or had she met my father who was living in Minneapolis, the twin city of St. Paul?

My father: My father, Norman, was also one of six children, two boys and four girls. His older sister did not come to the U.S. since she was already married when the family decided to leave Europe. Soon after the family arrived in Milwaukee, this daughter died (probably in childbirth) and her existing three children were brought to the U.S. by their grandparents, adopted, and took on the surname Radin. My father assumed the role of the eldest child and seemed to be the favorite of his siblings, particularly his sisters.

When I listened to my aunts talk about their parents, it was clear to me that they were a very close and attentive family. The household was full of other relatives who were likely to drop in for a visit. While they had not lived in a shtetl in Belarus (then called Byelorussia), the Milwaukee neighborhood where they lived took on the characteristics of that type of neighborhood. Many of the residents had arrived in the U.S. at the same time and built extended families drawing on both their families and neighbors for their support.

My grandfather died before I was born but all of his children spoke of him with great admiration. One of my aunts took me to visit the butcher shop which he had run; I have distinct memories of walking through the wood chips on the floor put there to avoid the smells. And these children treated my grandmother with respect and always made sure that she was comfortable. I never had a sense of what kind of person she was; she scrupulously went through the traditional daily prayers for women no matter where she was located. As the family spread out from Milwaukee, she visited her children who had settled in diverse locations. She didn't learn much English and wasn't really a part of the new American culture.

Because my father was already an adolescent when he came to the U.S., he evidently had difficulty moving into the U.S. educational system. I was told that both he and my uncle did not complete more than the sixth grade. Instead, they seemed to have taken their Americanization class seriously and developed both reading and writing skills in English that allowed them to move into the American world of work.

There appeared to be a lot of laughter and conversation in that household. At some point a piano appeared in the living room and the children were encouraged to develop musical skills. My father discovered the alto saxophone, an instrument he continued to play until his health did not allow him to continue (and then my brother took it over).

I remembered looking at the pile of sheet music that he had collected; most of the songs were popular in the 1920s and 1930s. And I have dim memories of members of the family gathered around the piano in song.

It is not clear to me whether my two oldest aunts graduated from high school but the youngest of the aunts did go to college. At some point, the other two aunts were trained as beauty shop operators and opened a hair salon. Many years afterward they continued to pull out their hair cutting equipment and volunteered to cut the hair of their nieces and nephews. The salon was effectively moved to the basement of the family house where one family lived on the first floor and another on the second floor. All three aunts adopted the American interest in playing the card game of bridge and continued that interest to become Master Bridge players.

My aunts seem to have adored my father. They described him as a very jolly, personable individual who could make friends easily. He enjoyed partying and conversing with individuals both in the house and outside. By contrast, his younger brother and he had a difficult relationship. My uncle did not appreciate the personal advice that my father gave without being asked. And my uncle tended to be more independent of the rest of the family and seemed to be out of the house more than in it.

For ten years this uncle kept a secret from his mother. He had a long-term relationship with a woman who was not Jewish and had married her. He asked his siblings to keep his secret although they did not agree with his secretive strategy. Evidently someone in the neighborhood knew about the marriage and told my grandmother about it. She replied, "If my son loves her, I love her." From that point on, my grandmother accepted her as a treasured daughter-in-law.

As a young child I became intrigued by my father's memories of life "in the old country." I pushed him to tell me stories about his life before coming to the U.S. and listened attentively to those tales. It took years before I realized that my father was recounting the stories from the work of Shalom Aleichem stories (a leading Yiddish author who had emigrated to the U.S.). When I discovered this, I was both annoyed at my father for misrepresenting his background but also impressed with his ability to draw on literature to satisfy my youthful inquisitiveness.

Given his personality, it was not surprising that my father sought jobs as a salesman. His sisters were convinced that he could sell anything, particularly if he believed in the product. I was told that he also enjoyed driving around the countryside as he sold his wares, often staying overnight at small hotels in the vicinity but returning home to Milwaukee as his base.

The stock market crash in 1929 and the subsequent depression made it difficult for both my father and his brother to find employment. But in the early 1930s he found a job with an investment company called Investors Syndicate (and eventually renamed Investors Diversified Services). Based in Minneapolis, the company sold installment certificates to the public allowing their clients to systematically save money. It was created in 1894 and eventually became one of the first mutual fund companies in the U.S. My father worked out of the Minneapolis headquarters but was assigned to a number of small communities in the general Twin Cities area. I think this was the first time that he lived on his own and when in Minneapolis stayed at transient places like the YMCA and small hotels. He was on the road constantly and became familiar with these small towns and their populations. The distance between Minneapolis and Milwaukee was not too far to preclude his regular visits home.

Despite the dire economic conditions, he seemed to thrive in this position. Probably his basic optimism allowed him to convince his clients that saving money was worthwhile. As a result, his sales record was good enough to get the attention of the top officials in the company. He seemed to be moving ahead and probably was thinking about the possibility of settling down and moving away from his bachelor life.

The Couple: I don't know when my father and mother met. Evidently it was at a party given by mother's brother who was a lawyer in Minneapolis. Given his gregarious nature, my father made friends easily. I pictured my parents meeting as two attractive individuals, both of whom were quite short, (my father was about 5'4" and my mother was about 4'11"). My mother was a red head who was friendly, bright and stylishly dressed. Probably her recent time in New York City gave her access to the most recent styles. My father was a dark haired man who was personable, also aware of current styles, and a good conversationalist. Neither was young by standards of the day. My father was in his middle thirties and my mother was in her early thirties. My father had recently become an American citizen.

The box of letters contained exchanges between my parents from January 1934 onward to the early years of their marriage. Their initial tone was more than casual but not intimate – a documentation of a conversation they were probably having during that period. Evidently they had spent time together after meeting at the party and learned quite a bit about each other. My mother was an enthusiastic correspondent; she wrote easily and was able to express her interest in my father's life. My father was comfortable sharing the details of his daily life with her as well. Just a month later (in February 1934) the letter from my father was addressed to "Darling." The relationship had changed. In March, my mother received a letter from my father's sister Rose (his favorite sister) and it was clear that the relationship had become serious. A letter written in April indicated that my mother had visited the Milwaukee family and met his parents and siblings. Because he was based in Minneapolis, my father had already spent time with my mother's parents across the river in St. Paul.

Someone in the family described the Milwaukee meeting between my mother and her future mother-in-law. It wasn't unusual for such a meeting to take on the characteristic of what has been called "Jewish geography" – a process where participants try to identify people they know in common. Although the two families had lived in different locations, they were both from the area between Minsk and Pinsk in Belarus. Evidently my mother described her grandparents and probably emphasized her mother's father – Rabbi Pinchas Goldberg (my great-grandfather) – since he was viewed as the most important of the relatives.

Rabbi Goldberg was characterized by one former resident of the town as someone who people consulted with questions, for advice, and to ask for his blessings. (Evidently the Rabbi was sometimes known as "The Miracle Worker of Romanova"). It turned out that my grandmother, as a young attractive woman, was one of those individuals seeking advice (for what I have no idea). The story goes that she found herself alone with the Rabbi and was very uncomfortable with the situation. She quickly left the meeting. I never could figure out what to make of that story. Was this ancestor of mine interested in this young woman or was my grandmother paranoid? But the incident became a part of the Radin lore and in some ways illustrated the differences between the two families. Although I always sensed a tension between my mother and my father's sister Rose, I also had the feeling that my mother enjoyed the warm feelings in the Radin household – somewhat of a contrast with the Edelman family where tension ran high.

The courtship was not long. While their meeting was likely to have been the result of family suggestions, there was no sign of a formal arranged marriage. The April 1934 offer of an opportunity to lead the South Dakota Territory office of Investors Syndicate gave the couple a chance to start a new life. In the environment of the depression, this was not an offer that one took lightly. My father had the responsibility of developing a staff and opening an office in Aberdeen, a small city of approximately 16,000 people, 300 miles directly west of Minneapolis on Route 12. While most often on the road, when in Aberdeen he lived at the local YMCA. He opened a box at the local Post Office for both his personal and business mail. That box – Box 557 – remained in the hands of the family until my mother left Aberdeen in the late 1960s.

Most of the letters of that early period could have been written by anyone of that era. The exchanges rarely reflected that they were immigrants or their religious background. A few of the letters contained Yiddish phrases and reference to classic Jewish food (such as "I miss your mother's borscht" – the cold beet soup that was a standard item in the cuisine of Russian Jews.) But those references were rare. A few of the letters were in Yiddish, written by the older generation of the two families. Both my mother and father almost always concluded their letters with "please send my best to your folks." As time went by, my father began to make friends in Aberdeen's small Jewish community and told my mother about possible people she could meet when they moved to the small city.

My father's letters belied the limits of his formal education. He expressed himself clearly in English and appeared to be able to communicate his experiences and feelings. The Midwest weather of the depression era was often the subject of the letters. My father once wrote, "What a storm we are having here. Nothing but dirt, dirt, no matter where you go. I'm waiting for the rain." My mother tried to figure out whether the weather moved from St. Paul to Aberdeen or visa versa.

My mother was likely to let my father know about items in newspaper clippings that might interest him. One clipping asked the reader who they would like to meet; my mother suggested that she'd like to meet Jane Addams (the Chicago based social worker who was a pioneer in settlement house reforms). A clipping on the World's Fair in Chicago in June turned out to influence their honeymoon plans. They both made reference to the possibility of the development of television and how they would have liked to see the other on a screen when they were apart. They would have loved Skype. They mentioned books they were reading and movies they would like to see. My mother was likely to offer a quote or two from either poetry or literature that she thought was appropriate. She also talked about taking tennis lessons and getting her racket back from New York City. Both of them were concerned about the health of the other and made suggestions about foods that might improve their health (such as Bulgarian buttermilk). When my father described his dinner of liver and bacon, it was clear that he did not observe Jewish dietary requirements.

My father was worried about his ability to deliver on the expectations of his Minneapolis bosses. One got the sense of life in the depression era from his concerns. He wrote about his potential customers, their resistance to systematically saving money, and sometimes calculated the amount of payment that he might receive (or lose) as commissions. He had the idea of recruiting local teachers as salesmen for the Investors Syndicate during the summer, believing that their educational background would give them the ability and status to educate customers about a somewhat complicated fiscal situation.

While my father usually wrote his letters on the road on stationary from hotels in the small Dakota communities, my mother wrote most of her letters from her parents' house in St. Paul. Sometimes she wrote the letters in longhand but often relied on her typewriter at home to express her views. I believe that she had purchased that typewriter in New York and brought it back to St. Paul with her. She would escape to her room in her parents' house to have a written conversation with my father. Occasionally she was concerned that typed letters were impersonal and did not communicate her real feelings. But she was very fluent composing comments on the keyboard. Her high school experience with essays showed through in these letters. (She was working as a secretary in a lawyer's office during this period.)

From April to August of 1934 when their marriage took place, the letters moved to focus on aspects related to the wedding. My mother picked up her engagement ring in July, purchased from a family acquaintance. My father began looking for housing in Aberdeen, describing an apartment in a building that was the best that Aberdeen offered. My mother described her shopping expeditions, using sales in department stores to collect linens and other staples for her new life.

Plans for the actual wedding were extremely modest. My father did not have vacation time. Since he relied on commissions, his extended absence from work would be financially problematic. The economic conditions of the period made it unlikely that the Milwaukee delegation could come. And my mother's father wanted to make sure that they were married by a rabbi before the Sabbath on Friday night. As the wedding date came closer, my mother's letters almost seemed like a list of questions interspersed with comments. About the same time, her New York City friends were notified about her coming plans. She received letters of congratulation from them; one commented that it seems "your restless urges are over." That was an observation that really surprised me since I had never envisioned my mother as "restless" although that would have been an appropriate adjective to describe my approach to life.

A number of the letters concluded rather hastily because the writer wanted to make sure that the letter got on the next train. There were regular trains between Aberdeen and Minneapolis/St. Paul. The letters seem to have been written by one or the other person every other day. Missing the train really disrupted the flow of the conversation.

My parents were married on August 30th, 1934 in a very small ceremony at the rabbi's house. A formal (and quite elegant) wedding announcement was sent by my grandparents noting that "Mr. and Mrs. Morris Edelman announce the marriage of their daughter Sophie Mattalie to Mr. Norman Radin on Thursday, August the thirtieth nineteen hundred and thirty-four, Saint Paul, Minnesota. At home The Dorian Apartments, Aberdeen, South Dakota." A copy of that announcement was included in the contents of the box of letters. Pressed between the pages of the announcement was a dried flower that was probably my father's boutonnière.

They were able to arrange a honeymoon at the World's Fair in Chicago and brought home a photo of the two of them at the Fair grounds. They seemed to be very happy. It is likely that they stopped in Milwaukee en route to Chicago to visit with the Radin clan since none of them were able to attend the wedding.

REDISCOVERING MY PARENTS

Until I read (and reread) the letters in the box I had not given much attention to the lives of my parents before they were married. At best, I had a two dimensional view of them and certainly did not link my personal development to their influence. Probably this was most pronounced in my view of my mother. As I was growing up, I perceived her as a very traditional woman who focused her attention on her children, home, and husband. It had not dawned on me to think about the dramatic change that she made in only a few months after moving from Manhattan to a small city in South Dakota. She came to a community with almost no contacts, no old friends, and an environment that lacked the cosmopolitan stimulation of New York City. Did she even consider who she would be able to talk to beyond my father in that new setting?

Her move a decade earlier from St. Paul to New York City had represented her adventure into a very different America, one that moved her away from her family and St. Paul. Her move to Aberdeen represented an emersion into yet a different America and probably made St. Paul seem very urban. It is hard for me to imagine how she found a way to deal with that change.

My father's life seemed to represent a less dramatic shift. Yet he had moved from a close knit family living in a Jewish neighborhood in Milwaukee to an environment of farmers, small town residents and individuals with very different backgrounds than his. The Midwest of the 1930s was suffering from the depression and the uncertainty that accompanied it clearly had an influence on his attempt to create a career. My memories of him were enriched by his letters, which provided a picture of a man who was able to communicate with people with diverse experiences and to find ways to assist them. Perhaps my favorite comment from one of his letters came when he visited South Dakota's state capitol, Pierre. He described the beauty of that small city and noted that, "I feel like a senator parading in the main street of the town."

Each of my parents found a way to blend their experiences as new immigrants to the U.S. with the opportunities that this country offered. I didn't realize it at the time, but that dynamic provided a model for me in the future.

CHAPTER 2
Aberdeen

I've often wondered how my mother reacted to her first glimpse of Aberdeen. She and my father probably drove from the Twin Cities along the main road – U.S. Route 12 – to enter the small city. The apartment they had rented was just a block or two off of Main Street, providing an easy walk to the shops for my mother who didn't drive. The apartment building was built in 1910; it was the only large apartment building in the city and was surprisingly urban in the small city. It was within walking distance of the local college, then called Northern States Teachers' College, and probably had a number of faculty members among its occupants.

Compared to the small towns that my parents probably drove through from Minneapolis to Aberdeen, Aberdeen did seem to be thriving. Named for Aberdeen, Scotland, the hometown of Milwaukee Railroad President Alexander Mitchell, it was incorporated in 1881 and quickly became known as the Hub City of the Dakotas, and the Brown County seat. It had one of the fastest growing populations in that part of South Dakota. By the turn of the 20th century, nine different rail lines converged in the city and the combination of multidirectional railways and fertile farmland caused Aberdeen to develop into a distribution hub for wholesale goods. In addition to its role in the regional railroad network, it was a jumping off point for homesteaders, and the core of regional education, fine arts and culture. To this day, the city is known as the home of L. Frank Baum, the author of the *Wizard of Oz* stories; he lived in Aberdeen from 1888 to 1891 and based his books on his experiences in drought-ridden South Dakota.

During the first year after their wedding my mother spent a fair amount of time going back and forth between Aberdeen and Minneapolis/St. Paul. Sometimes she accompanied my father to the Twin Cities when he had meetings at the Investors Syndicate headquarters. Since my father was usually on the road and she probably had made few friends in Aberdeen, she had a foot in both locations. She often stayed with her brother in Minneapolis and became very close to his growing family. The letters during that period suggest that my mother continued to use the Twin Cities as her base because of medical treatment. She consulted a doctor in Minneapolis before the wedding and seems to have continued with him afterwards. Neither my mother or father talked about children in their letters but I always thought they both wanted a family. A year after their wedding my mother gave birth to a stillborn baby. I don't know if she was consulting a doctor in Minneapolis and thus was in town for the birth or if her labor started unexpectedly when she was already in Minneapolis. She was hospitalized in Minneapolis for more than a week. She asked my father to bring some of her things from their Aberdeen apartment while she was in the hospital, including copies of *The New Yorker* magazine (for which she had a subscription). That was surprising to me, a serious devotee of the magazine. And when I realized that *The New Yorker* was only about ten years old at the time, I realized that my mother had good instincts about its future.

I learned about the stillborn baby when I was fairly young. I often fantasized about my "sister" and thought about life as a second child instead of being the oldest. That baby was buried in the Edelman family's St. Paul cemetery plot where my grandfather had arranged for the burial and the headstone for the baby. I don't think that either of my parents ever recovered from that experience. When I asked my father about my sister, he broke into tears. Responding to my question about the baby and the death of Franklin Roosevelt were the only two situations where I saw him cry.

I was born about fourteen months after the stillborn baby. My mother found a doctor in Aberdeen and I was born in the local hospital. During that time it seemed that my mother became more assimilated to the culture and people in Aberdeen. She used the small Jewish community in Aberdeen as her base, developing friendships that lasted the rest of her life. She had a distant cousin who was married to someone who lived in Aberdeen; that family tie became the basis for her future relationships.

Judging from the letters, my mother kept in touch with friends from New York City. One friend tried to envision my mother's life in the prairie, asking her in a letter whether she was able to meet people "in the clubs in Aberdeen" and another asked her whether South Dakota was like China. Years later, when I was in college, I had a running conversation with a friend from New York. Over and over again I told him that I was born in South Dakota and that I had spent my first eighteen years there. Yet he remained convinced that I was from New York, in fact from Brooklyn. Perhaps he too thought that South Dakota was like China. At any rate, I didn't fit his image of a Midwesterner.

MAIN STREET

Probably every Midwestern town of that era had a Main Street that served both economic and social functions. The main retail areas in Aberdeen were located in the blocks between the railroad station (to the north) and the major east-west U.S. highway crossing Main Street at the south. Depending where we were starting out, we would describe a visit to the shops and other establishments as going either "uptown" or "downtown." A walk north brought one past a furniture store, a grocery store, a department store, a shoe shop, a children's clothing store, and an array of women's ready to wear shops on both sides of the street. Interspersed between these shops were restaurants (including two Chinese restaurants), the Masonic Temple and several movie theatres. I think that the cost of a movie ticket up to the point when I went away to college was twelve cents. Less prestigious establishments such as army surplus stores were found the closer one travelled north to the train station. The county court house was located close to the railroad station as was the major hotel in the city. My father's office was located in the Citizens' Bank Building, across the street from the hotel; built around 1914, it was one of the very few multi-story buildings of the time that had an elevator.

Walking up Main Street was more than a shopping venture. At least half of the Jewish families in Aberdeen were merchants. That part of the community was linked to the states on the east coast through regular shopping visits by the store owners to buy up to date merchandise in Minneapolis, Chicago or even New York. Walking into a store often meant a visit with the owners (and sometimes their children). Until I went to college I didn't realize that everyone didn't receive a phone call from a shop's owner to let you know that something had arrived that you might want to purchase. While this was an interesting convenience (somewhat like having a personal shopper), it made me feel as if I didn't have any privacy. While I was in college, I came home for a long overdue visit (I hadn't been home for several years) and went to the local department store to buy some cosmetics. The person behind the counter looked up and said, "Hi Beryl. Haven't seen you for a while." That was an environment of predictability that I didn't want to experience in the future.

DIVERSITY

It was probably a result of the multiple railroad lines coming into town that Aberdeen's population at that time was quite diverse. There was evidence of social and cultural cleavages in the population of the town itself. A listing of the churches found within the city limits indicated many different Protestant congregations (Baptists, multiple Lutherans drawn from different Scandinavian populations, Methodists, Congregationalists, Presbyterians, and Episcopalians) and two different Catholic parishes. These two Catholic churches, each with its own primary school, represented very different communities. One was middle class with members who identified themselves as Irish Catholics (sometimes known as Lace Curtain Catholics). The second was drawn from people who had moved from farms to the "city" and came from German-Russian backgrounds. The latter were descendants of Germans who left Germany for Russia after the Reformation. That church was located a block away from the synagogue and I experienced taunts from children who attended the school attached to the church. These children would yell at me, "You killed Christ," and I wasn't sure what they were trying to tell me. At one point I responded, "I wasn't even there" since I couldn't think of any other response.

During my nearly eighteen years in the community there were no people of color except for one or two African Americans who played for the city's professional baseball team. There were, however, American Indians among the population, most of whom worked for the federal government's Bureau of Indian Affairs office in town.

Diversity also came through the farmers who came to town every weekend to shop. Aberdeen was the commercial magnet for the farming communities that surrounded it. Saturdays were bustling as farmers came to buy supplies and to sell their products. I was surprised to see the variety of farmers present, particularly those from the nearby communities of Hutterites (similar to Amish and Mennonites) who came to town dressed in long skirts, bonnets and other unusual garb. I knew that the children of those families were highly regimented and were not allowed to mingle with those of us in town. Some of the Hutterites had moved to town and settled in. They were no longer visually different from others in terms of their dress but were likely to oppose elections to support increased taxes for schools and for the library.

Aberdeen was the site of whatever federal government presence that could be found in that part of northeastern South Dakota. A new federal building was built in the 1940s (probably as a result of New Deal programs) that housed the Bureau of Indian Affairs as well as the Post Office and a few other federal agencies. And Brown County (the county in which Aberdeen was located) was almost always the only county in the state that regularly elected Democrats to the state legislature. The town perceived itself as open to change and able to keep up with developments in other locations. It was almost comical when the local government decided to turn a number of streets into one-way roads. Although one-way streets are designed to manage heavy traffic (something clearly missing from Aberdeen), it seemed that the decision represented the town's desire to keep up with current practices elsewhere.

When I was in junior high school, a close family friend, Abe Pred, was elected to the South Dakota State Senate from Brown County. Even at that age I realized that it was quite unusual for a Jewish person who was not a native of Aberdeen to serve in political office. He was elected as a Democrat for several terms from 1949 to 1953 and brought local politics into our household.

FITTING IN

Both of my parents established relationships that indicated their commitment to become a part of the larger community. My father was a member of the Masonic Lodge and also moved up to become a Shriner. It was a shock to me to attend the annual Shrine Circus production and see my father talk to one of the clowns (who was a local Shriner). I couldn't figure out how he knew a real clown. He also joined the Elks Club and took me to the club where I cultivated a great interest in slot machines. Both of these involvements were useful to his role in Investors Syndicate and were consistent with his gregarious personality. My mother became a member of the women's Masonic group, the Eastern Stars. And when I was old enough, I became a member of the girls' organization, Jobs Daughters. All of these organizations met in the Masonic Lodge in the middle of the shopping areas of Main Street.

It wasn't clear to me how my family fit into the Masonic structure. It seemed somewhat incongruous for a chubby Jewish girl to wear a Greek-style robe at the meetings and to be the pianist for the ceremonies. I also found it strange that Masonic policies did not allow Catholics to be members. Yet I knew that one of my friends who came from a Catholic family joined me as a member.

My mother took the responsibility of leading my Girl Scout troop and was active in the PTA group in the elementary school my brother and I attended. I began activity in Girl Scouting as a Brownie Scout at about seven years of age and stayed with Scouting throughout high school as a Senior Scout. That involved selling the infamous Girl Scout cookies to everyone I knew, going to Girl Scout camp for a few weeks during the summer, and learning how to prepare meals and build fires at the local park. My troop baked cookies to take to the train station for soldiers who were on the train going either east or west during World War II. Seeing those young men in uniform brought the war much closer to my life., and those images were reinforced by our next-door neighbors, a family that had three or four sons in the service and had already lost a son in battle. They had a banner in their window that proclaimed that the mother in residence was a Gold Star Mother, women who lost their son or daughter in the war.

Other parts of my childhood were linked to World War II. We had a fairly large plot of land that turned into a victory garden, the activity that encouraged residents to plant vegetables that could be used in the family. I was very aware of food shortages that were regulated by distribution of food coupons and coins that were required to be provided before purchasing food. I think that almost every family in town saved string and rubber bands. I remember riding my tricycle on the sidewalk the day that the war was over, making a celebratory noise with the bell on my cycle (I didn't learn to ride a two wheeler until I was twelve).

World War II wasn't an abstraction in our household. It was common for many children to be told that they would help the war effort by cleaning their plates at mealtime (thus being attentive to the food shortages that were a part of the war effort). In my family, my mother put a special spin on the ritual. Once we cleaned our plates we were allowed to take our fork to stick Hitler in the rear. I have never heard of others adopting that practice!

There were other ways that I learned to fit in. Every year my Girl Scout troop (along with other troops) serenaded the shoppers on Main Street with Christmas carols. From about Thanksgiving to the New Year, a bleacher was put up on the lawn of the Masonic Temple in the pyramidal shape of a Christmas tree. This became the "singing Christmas tree" for Girl Scouts. As a result, I still have a fairly extensive repertoire of Christmas carols. One of the high spots in the fall was the homecoming parade sponsored by the local college in celebration of Gypsy Days. The parade was patterned on the Rose Bowl event even though the bands and the floats weren't up to that standard. But everyone in town lined Main Street to participate in the celebration.

I learned how to escape to the basement of our house when the predictable tornados hit. I remember driving with my father to some of the small towns outside of Aberdeen the day after a severe tornado had occurred. I saw a bathtub sitting far away from what was left of a house and a piano in shambles in the same area. I thought about the possibility that something like that could affect my family but was reassured that tornados usually came in predictable paths and our house was not in one of them.

There was both an element of predictability and unpredictability about the weather in general. Summers were hot, dry, and prone to tornados. Winters were extremely cold (we were likely to go to school in temperatures of forty degrees below zero) with huge snowdrifts that resulted from the blizzards. For months in the winter those snowdrifts blocked our back door. And the months of spring found the local creek (Moccasin Creek) rising above its banks and creating floods in parts of the city before some reclamation projects were undertaken.

But on some level I knew that I wasn't really a part of the world of South Dakota. I knew I was different. I have a distinct memory of a second grade classroom where one of my classmates (upon hearing me say that I was Jewish) informed me that he knew I couldn't be Jewish because he had seen pictures of Jewish people in his Bible story books. He told me, "All of the Jewish people in those books wore robes. You don't wear a robe. I know you aren't Jewish." That episode – at age seven – is my first memory of something that seemed like anti-Semitism.

In many ways my life growing up was not much different from other kids in Aberdeen. There was a small zoo in the park outside of town that was a regular stop with my father. My brother and I loved seeing the buffalo herd (really bison) at the zoo roaming in the prairie land as they had when they were wild. After being taught to play the piano originally by my aunt in Minneapolis, I took lessons from a teacher who came to teach in the elementary schools. As I progressed I continued lessons from music faculty at the local college. As I grew older, I added the flute to my musical repertoire and joined the high school band and the orchestra.

I played the card game of hearts in the Y down the street with my friends. I hung out at the local drive-in and spent spare change on the pinball machines found there. I made regular visits up and down Main Street with my friends, stopping in a coffee shop after school where I learned to make straw covers dance by dripping Coca-Cola on them. During the summers when there was a lack of many activities, I joined my friends at the baseball park watching the Aberdeen Pheasants, the professional baseball team, and learned how to fill out the detailed scorecard of their performance. When the team was playing in other communities I listened to the tickertape radio coverage of their success or failure. I took school seriously but also seemed to excel in non-academic activities. I would tell my friends that I was majoring in extra curricular activities. In addition to musical activities, I also was involved with the student council and the school newspaper.

My comfort in school was probably related to attributes of the school system itself. I could never confirm this, but I was told that the Aberdeen educational curriculum had been developed in the 1930s by a superintendent who came to the community from the Harvard Education School. He left Aberdeen to become the superintendent of the New Trier School System, a suburb outside of Chicago. That system was viewed as one of the most important locations for progressive education methods in the country. As I grew older, I came to learn that it was not common to have a seventh grade class titled the "Core" course (that included shop, cooking, and sewing) where boys and girls learned these skills together in the same classroom. At the time, such a curriculum was viewed as radical. John Dewey's views about learning by doing also probably influenced my Latin class teacher's decision to require all of the class members to come to class one day wearing a toga. It was a strange sight.

THE ABERDEEN JEWISH COMMUNITY

If I had a point of identification in Aberdeen it was found in the small Jewish community. As I was growing up, the Aberdeen Jewish community was made up of approximately twenty families. Many of the families were involved in the ready-to-wear business clothing shops for women; some had quite elegant stocks and others catered to a more middle class or lower middle class clientele. One of the three movie theatres was owned by a member of the community. The local department store was owned by a family that had left Judaism to become Christian Scientists. Businesses that sold surplus military equipment (we called that the junk business) were owned by several members of the same family. Three branches of another family operated grocery stores in different parts of the town. It is my memory that only one member of the Jewish community was an active professional; he was a lawyer who came to the community and managed to be elected to a county judgeship. One man had been trained as an engineer but did not practice his profession. My father was the only person in an investment job.

Several of the merchants (or their families) had come to South Dakota as peddlers; they gave up their itinerant life to open stores in Aberdeen (and also in some other South Dakota communities). There were two families that somehow made their way from New York City to Aberdeen in the midst of the depression; they had relatives in town who found jobs for them.

Despite its limited size, the Aberdeen Jewish community had opened a synagogue in 1917. The B'nai Isaac Congregation was established on the north side of the city in a building that had been a Protestant church. The synagogue was located in a lower middle class area, just a block away from one of the two Catholic churches and schools in town. I do not know whether the congregation was able to employ a rabbi during its early years. By the time I was aware of things, a very elderly rabbi had retired and was replaced for a few years by another elderly refugee from the Holocaust. But it was the third rabbi, a German who was also a survivor, who played the most important role in my experience in the synagogue. He came to Aberdeen with his wife and three daughters and stayed for approximately a decade. He was the person who organized the after-school Hebrew School, Sunday School and other activities.

My memories of this rabbi are full of contradictions. I recognized his commitment to education and was especially fond of his wife who was a warm and interesting person. But he was also very Germanic in his mode of operation. He expected students to toe the line and to comply with his directives. One day during Hebrew School (I was about twelve years old) I was absolutely disgusted with his approach and informed him that he had methods like Joseph Stalin. I stomped out of the synagogue and went home. By the time I arrived home, he had telephoned my mother and told her that I had to apologize to him for my remarks. I refused to do so (even though I recognized that my outburst was inappropriate). He and I never discussed the episode. He moved to a larger congregation in Superior, Wisconsin.

While the rabbi played an important role, the community itself had a structure and life of its own that defined the way that the synagogue operated. The members of the congregation were very diverse in the way that they characterized their religious observances. The synagogue had joined the Conservative movement, largely because it was the middle ground between Reform and Orthodox observance. Congregation members were more likely to attend services on Friday night, rather than on Saturday mornings, because merchants found it easier to leave their places of business on Friday night than during the day on Saturday. Some congregants came to the synagogue grudgingly and resented any time they spent there.

As I observed the behavior of the congregants, I realized that there were actually four different groups within the small synagogue. The physical structure of the building defined the location of those groups, following the design of the original church. There were three sets of pews in the structure. The middle set was twice as wide as those on the left and right sides of the building. The congregants who sat in the front section of the middle cluster were those who felt comfortable with the Conservative approach to services. The individuals who sat in the back middle cluster (and grumbled about the length of the service and the sermon, wanting to get in their cars to listen to the Friday night boxing matches) really wanted a Reform service. There were two different groups who sat in the narrow clusters, both of which were Orthodox. In one of the groups, the men sat in the left front rows while their wives sat in the right back rows. The second group was reversed; the women sat in the right front and the men in the left back. In both cases, the men and women were separated and located as far from one another as was possible. I think that I learned about the complexity of organizations observing this behavior and the way it also described other aspects of the Jewish community. I later learned that there was a saying that if you had two Jews, you had at least three opinions.

Although my family was quite comfortable with the Conservative designation of the synagogue and the use of the Conservative prayer book, my rebellious attitude gave me another perspective on the services. We did sit in the front rows to indicate our identification with the rabbi but I spent much of the service imitating the rabbi as he took off his watch to time his sermons. Several of us had constructed a synchronized action where we took our watches off at the same time and put them on when the rabbi concluded his remarks.

But my real identification with the service rested with the two Orthodox groups of men. All of them were immigrants, most of them were Litvaks (from the area that shifted in designation between Poland, Russia and Lithuania) and their chanting of the service and dovening (the style of swaying while reciting the prayers) drew me in. To this day I can hear their voices and strong Litvak accents when various melodies are sung. Although I was supposed to be learning Hebrew in the Israeli-approved Sephardic pronunciation (the style of the Jews from the diaspora to largely Spanish and Portuguese areas), there was something about that Eastern European Ashkenazi (the style of the Jews from the diaspora to northern and central Europe) sound that I found more beautiful and moving. While it did have a guttural sound, its primitive power was very satisfying. The musical sounds that emerged from that place of worship were somewhat unusual – elderly men joined by one adolescent young woman. I especially enjoyed the practice of auctioning off portions of the Torah (the scrolls containing the five books of Moses) to read during Yom Kippur (the holiest holiday of the year); that process seemed to me both incongruous with the solemnity of the service but a wonderful performance nonetheless.

Despite my positive views about the services, I also recognized that the traditions had real limitations. My father died when I was ten years old and that meant that my brother and I would be the only children in the congregation who would be present at Yiskor (memorial services). If that was not difficult enough, I learned that my mother had an encounter with the leadership of the synagogue who did not believe that a daughter should be able to say Kaddish (the memorial prayer) for her parent. At that point, it was assumed that only sons could say the prayers. My mother insisted that both of her children should stand and say the prayer. That may have been one of the first signals I had that my mother had some feminist tendencies. I learned that this was not uncommon when I read Letty Cottin Pogrebin's similar experience in her book, *Deborah, Golda and Me: Being Female and Jewish in America.*

Although I had some reservations about the traditions, I was still very comfortable in the synagogue. Occasionally I was given the responsibility of leading services on Saturday morning. Because so few members of the congregation were present the rabbi gave me that opportunity. Indeed, it was very difficult to get a minyon (the requirement that ten men are needed to say most prayers). At that time; after his Bar Mitzvah (the Jewish coming of age ritual for young men who are thirteen years of age) my brother was annoyed when he received early morning phone calls to come to the synagogue to help make up a group of ten men. I resented not being counted in the minion and clearly saw the gender bias in the system.

The High Holidays provided a high point during the year. The Aberdeen synagogue and the community opened their doors to Jewish families throughout the region. Pews that were sparsely filled during the year were replaced by standing room only as families came from fairly long distances to join in the service. For years we had a regular houseguest during the holiday, a man originally from Vermont who owned a jewelry store in the state capital, Pierre. He came alone, without his wife. He usually spent his summer vacation in Vermont and thus arrived at our house with fresh maple syrup.

These days were especially enjoyable for teenagers. The small

Jewish population in the town meant that there were very few children of the same age in the congregation's families. In fact, there was only one other person my age, one the year older, and one the year younger. And my brother and one other person were two years younger. But on Rosh Hashonah and Yom Kippur there were often other children of one's age and it was a great timing for partying. Those friendships were sometimes continued at a Jewish camp in Wisconsin during the summer and at meetings of the B'nai Brith Youth Organization across the Dakotas and in other parts of the Midwest. And, of course, like many other Jewish communities, Aberdeen's High Holiday services were a time to display new clothes and outfits, most of them purchased from Jewish merchants.

During some years, the congregation built a sukkah (a temporary outdoor tabernacle) in which to celebrate the Succoth holiday (a holiday to celebrate the harvest). There was just enough land available adjacent to the synagogue to put up the traditional outdoors booth structure. By the time the holiday came about, the weather in South Dakota was moving toward winter. We shivered in the sukkah when we ate the evening meal but I loved the harvest decorations that adorned it. I don't think that any of the individual families built their own structures but enjoyed being in a communal setting. It was also common to have community seders during Passover at least for one of the nights led by the rabbi. Those seders were loud, boisterous and a lot of fun; I actually became intoxicated for the first time at one of the rabbi's seders.

At some point, the congregation decided that it was important to remodel the synagogue. A new entrance hallway was created partly to serve to keep the noise factor down in the sanctuary. (To this day I'm surprised when a congregation is quiet enough to allow one to actually concentrate on the service.) The remodeling also involved turning the dark basement into a useable party space. That is where my brother's Bar Mitzvah party was held. The Ladies' Aid organization was involved in the details of the basement renovation and its decoration and fittings. I had the opportunity once to read the minutes of several Ladies' Aid meetings; one meeting seemed to have revolved around an extensive debate over the brand of cleanser that would be used in the kitchen.

The secretary who wrote the minutes of the Ladies' Aid meetings clearly had a sense of humor and presented the debate in a satirical fashion. Her minutes were biting but I don't think that most of the women in the organization understood that she was really mocking their long discussion about the cleanser to be purchased. She had come to Aberdeen during the New Deal after participating in the Federal Writers' Project in New York City. I don't ever remember a conversation between this woman and my mother about New York City but I did get the sense that they were like-minded.

When I was about fourteen or fifteen, I was responsible for teaching the pre-school group in the Sunday school. I knew nothing about teaching but felt that these toddlers needed to do something that called on their imagination. We were talking about Moses and the destruction of idols. Since the synagogue kitchen had a good supply of cans of cleanser (following the decision of the Ladies' Aid group), I gathered about ten of the cans, lined them up, and then gave the children the opportunity to knock them down with a broom handle. It certainly communicated the idea of destroying idols and I think that they enjoyed the class!

The creation of the state of Israel had a major impact on the community. No longer were families limited to collecting coins to be put into the Jewish National Fund (known as the JNF) blue box or to buying certificates marking the purchase of trees in Israel. Up to that point, I joined hundreds of other Jewish children who were convinced that there were forests in Israel that they had purchased. After 1948 when the state of Israel was established, the sale of Bonds for Israel became a serious fund raising endeavor. There were yearly Bonds for Israel dinners and the small Aberdeen congregation held itself out as having one of the highest per capita contribution of funds in the country during the 1950s.

Just recently, the Israeli newspaper *Haaretz* had an article on a meeting of Chabad-Lubavitch rabbis in Brooklyn. They reported that Chabad (a worldwide movement that promotes Judaism and supports Jewish education) had a presence in forty-nine of the fifty states. The only state without a Chabad presence was South Dakota. Just as this book is going to press, Chabad has come to South Dakota. According to the article, this was because the Jewish population in the state was so low: 345 Jews out of an 840,000 person population. But the Aberdeen congregation was touted as one of the "three historic Jewish congregations" in the state. And the article reported that even without a rabbi, Friday night services were held whenever one of the few remaining couples was in town.

From the time she came to Aberdeen as a young bride, I think that my mother knew that it would be difficult to maintain all of the traditions and requirements of the households which she (as well as my father) had experienced. When people asked her if she kept kosher, she avoided answering the question directly. It must have been hard for my mother to figure out how to organize a Jewish household in a community where there were only twenty Jewish families. I did learn that when she arrived in Aberdeen, she decided to keep kosher and bought her meat at a butcher shop owned by one of the members of the Jewish community. One day she observed the butcher prepare the kosher meat on a wooden slab on which non-kosher meat was also prepared. She decided that it was pointless to pretend that meat was kosher and gave up that illusion.

However, the grocery stores owned by Jewish families did provide a way to purchase products that were familiar although they did not formally meet kosher restrictions. Rye bread was brought in by truck and train from Sioux City, Iowa (which had a sizeable Jewish community). For years I thought that everyone called a particular variety of rye bread "Sioux City rye." Other products came by train from Minneapolis and St. Paul. And of course there were stocks of foods that were delivered from those locations in preparation for Passover.

LIVING IN TWO WORLDS

While I wasn't aware of it at the time, I left Aberdeen for college continuing a process that was somewhat similar to that of my parents. As immigrants to the U.S., they sought a way to take on the attributes of the American culture that seemed available to them. At the same time they acknowledged the cultures and values that emerged from their family backgrounds. My mother's decade in New York City was her effort to move away from the life her parents had known. Their decision as a couple to live in a small town in South Dakota was effectively a commitment to their Americanization goals and a belief that they could succeed in a difficult economic situation.

But what seemed to be adventure and opportunities to my parents became a constraint to me. I grew up in Aberdeen and took advantage of the opportunities that were available in that community but my focus was on ways to move beyond Aberdeen's traditional ways. As my next steps indicated, ironically I was using opportunities embedded in the Jewish community and culture to leave South Dakota.

CHAPTER 3
The Household

My first memories are based in the house where my parents moved around the time my brother was born. We had moved away from the apartment building that they had occupied when they settled in Aberdeen. The house itself was located on a busy street (at least busy by Aberdeen's standards). In fact, the street was a part of U.S. Highway 12, which took one to Minneapolis. It was less than two blocks from Main Street and thus easy for my mother to walk to since she didn't ever learn to drive a car. It was only a few blocks from the local primary school. That school – the Adams school – was built in 1907 and torn down within the last decade or so. The house itself was probably built in the early years of the 20th century, as were many of the surrounding houses. Most of the houses in Aberdeen were constructed of wood and homes were usually two stories high with a useable basement.

Since I haven't been back to Aberdeen for many years I used Google Maps to find the current status of my childhood home. That was a huge surprise. The several blocks west of Main Street are now almost completely commercial. In fact, our house was the only remaining house on the block. While the environs around it have changed dramatically, it continues much like what I remember.

The location of the house was not particularly fashionable. And though many people in the Jewish community were close friends (we learned to call those individuals "aunt" and "uncle" even though there was no blood relationship) members of that community did not live nearby. Most of those individuals lived in newer homes in more prestigious neighborhoods.

Our proximity to Main Street meant that commercial establishments (e.g. a gas station and a cemetery memorial monument store) were close by. On one side of our house was an elderly woman who lived alone in her house (we called her Grandma Darling and were convinced she was a witch). In other words, we were afraid of her and believed that she had left pheasant bones out for our dog to discover. And since pheasant bones were viewed as poisonous, when the dog found them we had to whisk her away to the vet immediately.

Our neighbors on the other side were a couple who were Republicans and whose sons were all in the military. At least one of the sons had been killed during World War II and I wasn't sure how those neighbors felt about a war related to abstract views about justice. Since my parents were staunch Democrats and Jewish, I found these neighbors interesting and learned from their conversations that it was only Republicans who pronounced the President's name "Roo-sevelt" rather than "Roa-sevelt."

We did have several friends in the neighborhood. The family down the street had a son whose birthday was a day before mine. That family became quite close friends and became a support system for my mother. A Norwegian family lived across the alley from us. Their daughter became our babysitter and as the years went by, the family reached out to include us in their Christmas celebrations. I have yet to find butter cookies that matched those Christmas goodies.

We lived in that house as renters for nearly a decade. I never learned why my parents did not buy a house. They clearly spent money on other things that were portable. I decided that it was their way of saying that their tenure in Aberdeen wasn't permanent. Until my brother and I were of school age, we had help in the house. The first person I was aware of came every day to help my mother with the house and the children. She left to become a nun and the first Christmas after her departure she sent me a nun doll. The second person who helped in the house was around longer. Her name was Frieda and I was convinced that the song

"America the Beautiful" was about her since there was a line that proclaimed "let Frieda ring."

The house itself was comfortable. On the first floor it had a large living room, a separate dining room, a spacious kitchen with room for a large table, and what we called "the play room" – a room that was filled with children's books and games and a spare bed for visitors. The living room wasn't the space where both children could be found except on Sunday nights when we gathered around the radio to listen to Jack Benny and the other radio programs scheduled on Sundays. There was the ritualistic change from slipcovers on the sofa and chairs during the summer to uncovered furniture for the winter. Those rituals never made a lot of sense to me. In addition, I was puzzled by the labels on light shades of lamps that warned you not to remove them. The upright piano was my point of activity during the week and by the time I was around seven years old I was happy to do a daily routine of practicing.

We didn't use the dining room on a daily basis. It was reserved for birthday parties, holiday celebrations, and dinners for guests. The parties were the subject of my father's home movies and illustrated my mother's attention to the party details and food. It was always a production to get that table ready for use; protective mats were taken out of a closet and put on the table to make sure that the wood wasn't disturbed. There was also a subtle circular path on the rug under the table, memorializing the fairly regular chase between my brother and me that emerged from predictable disputes between siblings.

Much of our time was spent in the kitchen or in the playroom. The kitchen table was large enough to provide space for my Girl Scout troop (my mother was the troop leader) and allowed my friends to produce fairly decent goodies. The playroom also held the "mangle" – the machine used to iron flat items such as sheets and towels (this was the era before no-iron products). It was my responsibility to dust that room weekly. The bookshelves were filled with familiar books and I often found myself lured to reread them rather than do my dusting chores.

The second floor had a large master bedroom and two smaller bedrooms. The only bathroom in the house was also on the second floor. It was large with a big tub and no shower and a closet for towels and bathroom necessities. The closet in the master bedroom was filled with an array of interesting objects belonging to my parents. Because Aberdeen was the center of pheasant hunting during the autumn hunting season it wasn't surprising that my father kept his hunting rifle hidden in the closet. While hunting was not a sport common to Jewish immigrants, it was a way for him to show that he was comfortable with the local practices. My mother's section of the closet included several long ball dresses that she put on occasionally for special events. I was always fascinated by them. Those dresses probably represented her desire to "fit in."

My brother and I were assigned to the other two bedrooms. I have a distinct memory of lying down for a nap in the afternoon when I was about four years old. My brother was already sleeping and my mother wanted me to follow suit. She lay down on the bed with me and within a few minutes she fell asleep. I waited until I was assured that she was really sleeping and left the room to go downstairs to play. I never found it easy to nap in midday; probably, I thought that I might miss out on something if I was sleeping.

The basement was not finished but had a separate toilet; a washing machine and tubs that could be used to hand scrub the wash; and the hot water heater and the oil burner. In addition, there was a small gas stove that my mother used to burn off excess feathers from chickens. I never liked going to the basement. It seemed creepy to me but when there were tornado scares one retreated to it. There was a trap door to the backyard that one could use to escape tornadoes. There were clothes lines in the backyard that were used on a regular weekly basis since few people at the time had dryers to go along with their washing machines.

FURNISHING THE HOUSE

Although the house did not look unusual from the outside, I learned from my friends that it was not usual from the inside. As I think about it now, my mother had brought a cultivated eye drawn from both her experience in New York City and her interest in sculpture to her decisions to furnish the house. She described a small bench in the living room as something in the Duncan Fyfe style. She was proud of the dining room and master bedroom furniture sets that were New England style maple. She had several Oriental rugs from her New York City employment. Other pieces of furniture in the dwelling were not usual for a South Dakota house.

But the main idiosyncrasies that were the subject of comments from my friends had to do with the size of the book library and the art that was found on the walls and shelves of the house. "I've never seen so many books" was a typical response from visitors on entering the house. Books were found on the shelves and surfaces throughout the house. Children's books were purchased and found in the playroom, housed in modern bookshelves painted yellow and red. They ranged from the traditional collections of fairy stories to age-appropriate books for girls and boys (including Bible stories and books about Jewish holidays). My favorite book was *When Sally Goes Shopping Alone*, a book that told the story of a young girl shopping by herself for a gift for her mother. Its message of independence and shopping continues to resonate with me. A colorful linoleum rug appeared in the middle of the playroom with a hopscotch design inviting play. A hobbyhorse that we named Black Beauty occupied that room until we became too big to use it. Books from the public library joined those we owned. Particularly during the summer the nearby public library was my destination and I always checked out the maximum number of books that the library allowed.

There was also a fairly large number of books in my parents' collection. My mother's books included volumes on Oriental rugs, fiction with Jewish themes, historical Jewish books, and picture books dealing with women's history and issues. My father (someone who had minimal formal education) was fond of reading about astronomy, comparative religion and often science fiction. Those books were sprinkled between the living room and his bedside table.

Visitors to the house also noticed the art that was on the walls and the objects on the shelves. In my experience, that was very rare for homes in Aberdeen. There were original paintings that my parents had purchased on their trips; among them was a dramatic oil painting of a gypsy woman, a painting of a South Dakota scene, and several watercolor still life paintings by a distant cousin in San Francisco. Lithographs of Humpty Dumpty scenes were found in our bedrooms to illustrate favorite nursery rhymes. There were some photographs of family members but they were relatively rare. My parents had commissioned quite elegant and artistic photographs of my brother and me that were hung in their bedroom. I was always attracted to the objects displayed on the bookshelves in the living room, especially a beautiful carved Chinese ivory box and a Chinese jade candlestick. Those two live on my shelves today.

Various items from exotic places surfaced in the house. My brother and I received authentic Sioux Indian costumes one year and paraded through the neighborhood wearing them. One could be assured that my parents – especially my father – would bring back interesting items from their trips. A wool plaid small blanket appeared, providing me with wool fringes that gave me a chance to practice braiding. My mother's good taste was also found in the "good" china and other fine dining ware. I doubt whether anyone else in Aberdeen had an art deco design martini shaker or a delicate Chinese luncheon set with a geometric design.

Behind the house was a very large yard that contained a swing set and an inviting lawn. A garage backed into the alley. I have a dim recollection that the garage held an old Model T Ford that my father was unwilling to part with. The yard itself was fenced in with a wire fence to delineate the boundaries between our house and that of the next-door neighbors. The yard was large enough to allow us to organize a croquet set. That probably was the extent of our physical activity in that area. The fence proved dangerous to various pets. We were often given baby chicks and ducks as gifts during Easter season. Usually they did not live very long but one set of the pets managed to live through the spring. They grew out of their original dyed feathers and thus acquired a bizarre look. They tried to escape from the yard but we found several of them had been caught in the fence and died.

On the left side of the house (where there is now a driveway) was an expansive garden. I have wonderful memories of picking food from that garden, particularly during the Victory Garden days of World War II. We had the usual vegetables: carrots, beets, tomatoes, and corn. During the summer we often picked tomatoes and corn just before lunch, cooked the corn for just a few minutes, and served it with sliced tomatoes. No other lunch has ever topped those fresh tastes. We also had a generous supply of rhubarb that seemed to reproduce itself without much assistance from us. I'm still a big fan of rhubarb sauce and pie.

The area around the house was planted with flowers and bushes. One knew that spring had really arrived when the lilac bushes bloomed and summer was announced by the appearance of hollyhocks (its blooms were always turned into dolls). My mother seemed to enjoy working in the gardens and getting her hands into the dirt. I don't know if she ever had a chance to do that earlier in her life. In my mind, being a gardener was not a Jewish activity although the Zionist effort to reclaim land in Palestine created an interest in farming.

But given the climate in Aberdeen, one was more likely to confront winter in our yard. The side door of the house opened to a space that became our answer to Alaska. We looked forward to blizzards because they provided us with adequate snow to build snow forts as well as snowmen. We waited until there was enough snow to construct a structure with steps, providing a way for us to run our cocker spaniel Daisy up and down the steps, over and over again. We managed to replicate that process when we spent some of our summer vacations on a lake in Minnesota where we ran to the edge of the dock, pushed the dog into the water, watched her swim back, and then duplicated the process again and again. That dog didn't have an easy life in our house although we really loved her. Because we lived on a busy street, Daisy had several encounters with the cars racing by. One year she was hit by a car and suffered a broken jaw. The vet wired up her mouth and I discovered that her mouth looked just like mine since I wore braces on my teeth.

Our house on Sixth Avenue was also unlike the homes of my aunts and uncles on the Radin side of the family. When we visited them in Milwaukee I was struck by the differences in the way that the two parts of the family organized their lives. They seemed to have both the values and the décor found in other houses in their West Side of Milwaukee

Jewish neighborhood. That was a neighborhood of two stories, two family houses that were similar to one another both in design and in inhabitants. The all-Jewish neighborhood (and its lack of diversity) had an impact on me and probably led to my concern about race and discrimination in later years. It was uncomfortable for me to see the poverty in African American neighborhoods as we took the bus downtown. And I found it difficult to hear some members of the family make what seemed to me to be racially insensitive remarks in their conversations. It wasn't consistent with what I had been led to believe. I had what was called a "Topsy Turvy Doll" – a double-headed doll with a black doll at one end and a white doll at the other with a reversible skirt covering the other head. It seemed to me that my doll was meant to represent similarities between the two races.

LEAVING THE HOUSE ON 6TH AVENUE

When my father died when I was ten years old, my mother decided to wait until I was ready to finish junior high school before moving. She knew I didn't want to change schools midstream. I did commute to the old junior high school for one year, taking advantage of a school that had absorbed the progressive education approach of a past school superintendent. The principal of that school taught several classes and had a very unusual approach to self-government expected of the students in his class. He usually required students to vote on various issues and assignments. He had a rule that if someone was nominated for a position, that person had to vote for himself or herself. He told us that if you didn't want the job, you shouldn't have allowed yourself to be nominated.

Although my parents had rented a house up to that point, my mother decided (upon the advice of her brother) to purchase a home. She found a house on the other side of Main Street that was similarly accessible to someone who didn't drive a car. Like the 6th avenue house, this house was also a wooden structure but was significantly smaller than the earlier place. Because of its location, it too was in a non-traditional residential area. We were next door to a gas station, across the street from a church, and on a block that didn't have other houses. Yet we were just a block away from Main Street and its shops and across a street from another church and other houses. The public library and the local YMCA (with a swimming pool and other activities) were close by and it was a bike ride to the college where I took piano and organ lessons. I did have friends who lived a few blocks away but no one I knew was in the immediate vicinity.

In many ways the location of that house was a metaphor for our life. We were a part of Aberdeen but didn't fit into the normal modes of identification within the community. We lived in a non-residential area. Not only were we Jewish but we were a family without a father. And my mother had purchased that dwelling, changing the pattern of renting that she and my father had established. The most interesting residents in the area were relatives of bandleader, Lawrence Welk; his brother lived across the alley from us.

The living room and the dining room in the house were about half the size of that in the earlier house. The piano was located in the dining room, against a wall between the dining room and the kitchen. The dining room table became the space for homework and projects. I was in the generation of children (pre television) who always had the radio on when doing my homework, drowning out any human contact or interference. The kitchen, too, was about half the size of its predecessor. It did not provide room for projects undertaken by my Girl Scout troop but did have room for a kitchen table that created eating space for meals for the three of us. The hallway to the backdoor had shelving that provided additional space for canned foods.

The furnishings throughout the ground floor came directly from the other house but the limited space meant that some of the larger pieces did not make the move. Many items – particularly the artwork and knickknacks – made the space familiar and comfortable.

Before one entered the front door of the house, guests (and inhabitants) walked through a porch room that held a bed, a treadle sewing machine (that I think came from my grandmother's house in St. Paul), and bookshelves. While that porch room was not heated and thus not really a space that was useable during the winter, it expanded the useable space during the other seasons. My strongest memory of that porch area came from an episode with my brother one cold winter day. While we had a pattern of chasing each other around the dining room table in the other house, there wasn't room in the new dining room for that behavior. But we still had the urge to battle in some way. So one day when my mother was not home, my brother pushed me into the porch area and locked the door between the porch and the living room. It was very cold and I wasn't dressed for that temperature. I started pounding on the glass window at the top of the door and within seconds smashed the window and saw that I had cut myself rather badly on the broken glass. My brother immediately switched roles, worked to stop the bleeding and brought bandages to my wound. When my mother returned, we both told her that the glass in the door had broken because of a slammed door. Neither of us ever told her what had happened. I still have a scar from that episode.

There was a small yard behind the house with room for a clothesline, a container to burn trash, and garbage cans. Along the side of the house was space for a vegetable garden that my mother enjoyed. The back door to the house was just a few steps down from the kitchen. During severe winters that door became immobilized because of snowdrifts from blizzards. And often the windows on the first floor of the house were covered completely by the snowdrifts. The basement to the house was accessible from that same set of steps. I had a strong sense of identification with the characters in *Little House on the Prairie*.

The upstairs was very modest. There were two bedrooms; I shared a bedroom with my mother while my brother had his own room. During warm weather I claimed the bed on the front porch as my bedroom. And – like the other house – we all shared one bathroom that was located on the second floor. It was not easy to work out bathroom schedules for an adult and two adolescents.

My mother changed from a full-time homemaker to someone who was trying to continue at least some of the work contacts that my father had made. She did go into the office from time to time but made contacts with possible investors and usually met them in their homes. It was hard for me to see her as a professional woman even though she joined organizations that put her in touch with women who were independent and on their own. Although I did know that she had worked for ten years in New York City before marrying, I didn't ever think of her as an independent woman.

There were, however, significant changes in our lives. It became more usual for us to come home after school to an empty house. Increasingly, however, extra curricular activities kept us at school after class hours and we arrived home later, just before dinner. I remember being worried during the winter when I would arrive home and my mother wasn't there. I had read too many Laura Ingall Wilder books and was convinced that my mother was lost in the blizzard. Sometimes, I thought of myself as the adult when I worried about her.

SCHOOL AS MY CENTERPIECE

The new house was quite close to the high school (for me) and the junior high school (for my brother). Even during the winter months the walk to school wasn't overwhelming. Central High School in Aberdeen was known for its music program, almost competitive in interest with the football and basketball teams. I not only played the flute and piccolo in the band but the flute in the orchestra and accompanied the chorus on the piano. That schedule meant that I arrived at school an hour before regular classes began and stayed after the classes ended. In addition to the music activities I also was involved in the Student Council, the school newspaper, and various clubs. Outside of school I also continued to be involved in Girl Scouts and Jobs Daughters and various activities that emanated from the synagogue.

The band director was probably the most notable – probably infamous – member of the high school faculty. He had been a member of the U.S. Marine Corps Band, the military band that was viewed as the most professional of the service musical groups. He believed that his high school band members should abide by the same structured expectations that he experienced in the Marine Corps. He used humiliation as his tried and true way to get the attention of the band members and found ways to draw attention to individuals who made mistakes or couldn't keep time.

One of his favorite lines was used when various instruments were out of rhythm. He called that situation "a piano player's convention," referring to the failure of piano players to abide by structured time but go off in their own direction. Whenever he made that crack he looked directly at me (since he knew I was a piano player as well as a flutist). After receiving this comment several times, I cooked up an arrangement with a friend who was a percussionist and played the tympani (kettle-drum). The tympani's pitch was the lowest of any of the instruments in the band. And my instrument – the piccolo – was the highest pitch. We decided that my friend would tune his tympani flat and I would tune my piccolo sharp. That meant that the sound that emerged from the band would be very dissonant and, as we thought, drove the director crazy but he never really figured out where it came from.

Another time the band director became obsessed with the uniforms worn by the band members. His standard was that the band members would look as professional (and military) as the Marine Corps Band. The available uniforms were not always in the sizes that the students required. I particularly had problems with my hat – it was too big and I was concerned about it flying off my head during band maneuvers during the intermission of football games. I decided to stuff the hat with toilet paper, allowing the hat to stay on my head. Unfortunately the football game was held during a very windy day and the intermission maneuver was in midstream when the wind blew off my hat. Not only did I lose the hat but the toilet paper came out of the hat and billowed down the field. The band director was not happy.

My exposure to music was not limited to the school building. In the late 1930s the Aberdeen Civic Music Association (later Aberdeen Community Concert Association) was organized when a representative of the National Civic Music Association and a number of interested citizens met to discuss the possibility of forming a local concert association under the auspices of the national organization in order to provide a series of regularly-scheduled, high-quality concerts to music enthusiasts in the Aberdeen area. That same year a new theater with a capacity for an audience of 1,500 provided a performance setting for visiting concert artists as well as audience members. During the group's early years, its concert seasons included artists of international renown such as Marion Anderson, Andres Segovia, Isaac Stern, Victor Borge, Ferante and Teicher, The Vienna Boys choir, The Cincinnati Symphony and Ballet Russe. As I grew older, I was more and more amazed that I had been able to see performances of individuals of that caliber in Aberdeen.

I was an attentive student in the academic part of my school day. I was particularly focused on history and a course entitled Modern Problems. I was fond of saying that I liked the Modern Problems class because I was actually a modern problem. I did see myself as someone who was not willing to comply with local norms. At the same time, my academic work was just fine and when I graduated I received a scholarship from a local businessperson that would contribute to my future college tuition.

I had a few friends in high school who came from small towns outside of Aberdeen that did not have high schools available in their school systems. I envied them because their families had allowed them to enroll in high school in Aberdeen and live in an apartment in town on their own during the school year. I couldn't wait to leave home and be on my own.

THINKING ABOUT THE FUTURE

By the time I graduated from high school, my focus was clearly away from Aberdeen. During summers I had gone away to camp (a Zionist camp in Wisconsin) and thought about what I would do next. I had attended B'nai Brith Youth conferences in North Dakota and in Chicago. And visits to family members in Minneapolis and Milwaukee shifted my gaze eastward. I knew that I wanted to attend college in that direction but I wasn't sure where that might be.

CHAPTER 4
Health and Death

It is well known that when one reaches the age of seventy the conversations between friends often deal with issues of health and, too frequently, acknowledgement of the death of friends and family members. Those subjects bring up other issues. When that happened to me I thought it was simply a result of my advancing age. But my attempt to reflect on my life uncovered a somewhat different explanation. I realized that I had grown up in an environment where these difficult subjects were a part of my earlier experiences.

The box of letters that I had discovered revealed that concern about health issues was a topic that found its way into the exchange of letters between my mother and father in the early days of their relationship. Neither of my parents seemed to take good health for granted and always inquired about the other's health. It seemed that my mother had left New York City temporarily because of illness a few years before she left there permanently. There were no clues about the nature of that illness and I am still not sure why she returned to her home for a relatively short time. My father's family's concern about health issues actually drove them to leave for the U.S. My paternal grandfather died relatively young (before my mother came into the picture) and his bronchial and respiratory problems seemed to have been inherited by subsequent generations. And the stillborn death of my sister just a year after my parents' marriage generated a continued concern from them about issues dealing with health and medical treatment.

MY FATHER AND HEART ATTACKS

The health of my parents – especially my father – became a major part of my life very early on. In February 1939, my father attended a work conference in New Orleans and while there sustained a major heart attack. My mother did not accompany him to that meeting since my brother had been born just a few months earlier. My father was hospitalized for more than a week and an exchange of letters between my mother and the New Orleans doctor made it clear that this was a significant health problem. The doctor wrote my mother: "There is no doubt but that he had a heart attack which seemed very grave at the outset, but the rapidity of progress made by the patient at this time would lead one to think that this attack was not as grave as was thought at first." My father evidently wanted to leave New Orleans and stop en route home to see relatives in Columbus, Georgia and in Milwaukee but the doctor was skeptical about that possibility.

A week after the first exchange of letters, the doctor wrote my mother that my father "was practically and completely over this last heart attack." The doctor had given him permission to stop in Columbus and to break up the trip. He noted, "I emphasized three important duties, which I think are imperative that he continue in a health state and I will mention them to you so that you may help me in keeping him well." The doctor spelled out these duties: "First, he should not gain any weight. Second, his biggest meal should be at noon time, while his supper should be very light, food such as cereals, soft boiled eggs, mashed potatoes or cream cheese and a light dessert such as Jell-O, ice cream or cup custard. The third, it is imperative that he have at least one hour's rest after his noon meal in order to break up the day. The nights that he goes out for social activities, he should rest at least two hours after his supper."

While these requirements seemed reasonable, they did not mesh easily with my father's work and the structure of his personal life. His work required him to drive long periods of time to arrive at the small towns and farms in South Dakota and to organize his schedule around the availability of potential customers. He usually stayed overnight in small hotels around the state where the restaurant menus were limited. And, he was someone who loved food and did not find it easy to abide by the doctor's suggestions.

I was only two and a half years old when he had this first heart attack. I really was conscious of his health issues later after he had subsequent heart attacks in the later years when he was hospitalized in Aberdeen. I remember visiting him in the hospital and actually learned to knit from some relative while we were sitting at his bedside. That was the time when everyone was knitting items for men in the military so I contributed to that cause.

I do not remember specific conversations in the family for the next five to eight years about his health. It is likely that those conversations took place only between my parents. I do remember writing a note to my father when I was about seven years old, asking him not to yell at my mother. As I think about that now, it is probable that those arguments were about his inability to conform to the medical suggestions. It is also likely that the World War II strictures on food availability may have limited my mother's ability to obtain the kind of food that he required. In addition, restrictions on the availability of gas for the car constrained his ability to drive to the areas in the state where customers might be identified. He did manage to find adequate gas to go to areas outside of Aberdeen to visit potential customers and also to visit farmland that he had purchased earlier. I remember going with him and my brother to visit one farm that was nearby. It wasn't easy to get to that location in the early spring where roads were muddy and difficult to travel. Once there, I ran out of the car to investigate what was available and quickly was chased by a very large pig that didn't think I had any business in his territory. He probably thought that anything that was muddy was part of his turf. I still am apprehensive about bumping into pigs. Luckily my subsequent life didn't put me in much contact with them.

From the perspective of a young child, not much changed during this period. I went to school. We continued our Sunday trips to the zoo. I took my piano lessons seriously. We celebrated birthdays (since my brother and I had birthdays eight days apart, we often had joint parties).

But when I looked at the home movies taken during that period, it was clear that my mother was worried. She visibly aged but tried to keep the structure of the family going. That involved entertaining my father's corporate officers who came to Aberdeen for pheasant hunting during the fall. My parents also attended functions sponsored by his Masonic lodge and I loved to go to my mother's closet to examine her formal dresses for Masonic dances.

We lived through the polio epidemic and spent several summers avoiding crowds by playing only in our back yard. One summer I decided that we should treat the books in our house as a library. My brother and I had three-by-five cards that we made into our own book catalogue with a separate card for each book. Since we had a fairly extensive collection of books, that project took significant time and probably got us through most of the summer. I had the idea that anyone who wanted to read a book had to sign for it and check it out.

In the late fall of 1945 between the end of the war in Europe and the surrender of Japan, my father decided to take a train trip to Madison, Wisconsin to visit his oldest sister, Rose. While there he sustained his final heart attack. It evidently was clear that this heart attack was serious and my mother, brother and I immediately went to Madison. I'm told that the kind of heart attack that my father experienced is the type that today would provoke heart surgery and would likely be successful. At that time, however, such surgery wasn't available and my father lingered in the hospital for several months. It was long enough that my mother and aunt decided that we should enroll in the local elementary school for the duration. I had spent time in Madison a few years earlier during a visit with my aunt and knew what it had to offer; I especially loved going to the well-stocked local zoo, which surpassed the small Aberdeen zoo. Both my brother and I were there during our November birthdays. I was ten and my brother was eight. My father died in mid-December.

It was common in Jewish families to try to insulate children from serious illnesses. At one point I wanted my mother to come to my Madison school for our holiday performance but my uncle told me that I shouldn't push her on that "since your father is dying." That off the cuff remark did scare me. That was the first time I learned about the seriousness of his illness and the first time I was aware of the pending death of someone close to me.

The family gathered for my father's funeral. But a decision was made by my mother that neither my brother nor I would attend the service. As I have learned, that was not unusual. What was unusual was a conversation that my brother and I had with my mother before the funeral. We were clearly upset not only because of my father's death but also because of the uncertainty we felt about our future. We sat down with her and asked her to promise to do two things: not to get remarried and not to move away from Aberdeen. She agreed to our requests.

LIVING WITHOUT A FATHER

I don't remember what I felt when we returned to Aberdeen after the funeral. I do know that for years afterward, I really didn't believe that my father was no longer alive. His travelling schedule had always meant that he was often absent from the house. Perhaps that explains my ability to deny his death. I immersed myself in school and in my piano lessons. My mother didn't want to interrupt my regular piano practicing schedule. I found it very convenient to practice after dinner to avoid doing the dishes. Of course she didn't want to interrupt her creative daughter even if it meant that there was more work for her. A photo of my father lived on top of the piano so I could think about his pleasure in my piano prowess. I don't think that I really acknowledged his loss until I left home for college.

The structure of our family had followed classic Oedipal patterns. I was my father's daughter and my brother was my mother's son. Both of us benefited from indulgent relationships with our respective parent. My father was the source of new dolls, new clothes, and other goodies for me. My brother developed asthma when very young and my mother was always concerned about his health. As the younger child, he was far more easygoing than I was and also did not need to wage the battles that I had already pursued. My brother's asthma caused my mother a lot of anxiety and she sought to protect him from experiences that might generate an attack. I did begin to see a pattern in those attacks that were both environmentally and psychologically based when he seemed always to have an attack around the Yom Kippur holiday. Granted that pollens were active during the early autumn, I also knew that he didn't like to go to synagogue for that holiday.

While I may not have absorbed my father's death, I did feel as if I were the odd person out in the new structure of my family. As I moved into adolescence I felt the need to develop a support system outside of the home. My brother spent time with my father's brother and his wife and accompanied them on their long trips to the west. While I had a fairly close relationship with my mother's brother in Minneapolis, it did not involve the trips that my brother took that seemed to me to be quite exotic.

I reached out to my aunts, my Aberdeen friends, and through summer experiences at camp developed friendships with people from other places. That certainly did not lead to a close relationship with my mother. In fact, I sought ways to avoid direct communication with her. Perhaps the most dramatic example of this difficult relationship came during my senior year in high school. A statewide chorus was chosen to perform at a conference out of town and I was asked to be the piano accompanist for the performance. The state of my communication with my mother was very tense and I didn't know how to tell her about this honor. Our communication patterns were difficult, at best. Instead of telling her directly, I told my brother and asked him to tell her. It is quite likely that she was hurt by this encounter.

There were times when I felt that I was the only person in the world who didn't have a father. There were many things in my life that differentiated me from my classmates and friends; the fact that I was Jewish was clearly one of them. But I was reminded of my different status in a number of ways. Occasionally there were father-daughter events that I couldn't attend that were particularly difficult. Those events clearly made me feel like an outsider.

For the next five or six years after my father's death two family members also died who had been important to me. First was my mother's father – the grandfather who had been brought to the U.S. to run the

St. Paul Talmud Torah. While I couldn't really communicate with him because of his limited English and my lack of knowledge of Yiddish, I thought of him as a warm and loving individual who was willing to reach out to his grandchildren. Soon after he was dismissed by the Talmud Torah, he lost his bearings. He wandered off and lost his independence. His children decided that he should move to the St. Paul Jewish Home for the Aged. He was there for a short time before he died.

The second death was that of my Aunt Miriam, the wife of one of my mother's brothers. As a child I thought of her as the mother I didn't have. She was a pianist and a music graduate of the University of Minnesota. She was the person who started me out with piano lessons and always seemed willing to listen to my issues. She was the person who told me about Antioch College and, as a result, I took that advice very seriously. When the time came for college applications, I followed her suggestion. She had a daughter who was four years older than I was and who, I later learned, always believed that her mother felt closer to me than to her.

While I didn't go to my grandfather's funeral, my brother and I went to Minneapolis for my aunt's funeral. My mother was already in Minneapolis to be with her sister-in-law who was in the hospital and when she died (during Passover) my brother and I took the train to join her. I still remember that train trip. It was a period when I was taking Jewish customs quite seriously so I prepared matzoth sandwiches to eat on the train. Our attempts to eat those sandwiches generated a great mess and we arrived in Minneapolis covered with crumbs.

The funeral and the process of sitting shiva (the Jewish memorial ritual in the home) in my aunt and uncle's home were one of the few times that I saw one of my mother's sisters who lived in Utah. Of the six children in my mother's immediate family, only my mother and my Minneapolis uncle had children. Thus I only had three first cousins on that side of the family. My aunt and uncle's children were not close in age when their mother died; one was about nineteen, one was a year younger than I was, and one was around seven. It was more overwhelming for a widower to be left with children, particularly one as young as seven, than it probably had been for my mother. But I was so overwhelmed by the loss of my aunt that I did not focus on its impact on her children. I realized later how difficult it was for the youngest child to deal with the loss of his mother but I didn't have the ability to empathize with his situation at the time.

A SINGLE PARENT PERSPECTIVE

My mother was widowed when she was in her mid forties. For more than a decade after her marriage and move to Aberdeen she had moved into a very traditional marriage role. Despite her experience in New York City before marriage, during those ten years she defined herself as a wife and a mother. I think that she had relied almost entirely on my father for financial plans even though his health issues should have provided her with concern about the future. My father's firm did find a way to make sure that my mother continued to get his commissions but they also created a position for her on the company's staff. While her personality was not that of a salesperson, she found a way to sell savings plans and mutual funds to women in town, particularly to teachers and other professionals. The extent of her business, however, was never clear to me.

I do know that I worried about money. It probably was the clearest expression of my feelings of abandonment. I knew that my mother did not feel comfortable about managing money and that our financial status had been controlled by my father. I didn't know what my mother would do without him. One of my Girl Scout projects involved devising a budget that would allow me to plan how to spend my allowance. At some level, I thought I had to learn about that and to take money seriously. Over the years I discovered that I had the ability to think about developing budgets not only for my personal needs but also in work situations. It resulted in a series of situations where I was comfortable dealing with financial issues.

I was not very empathetic about my mother's insecurity about money. As I think about it now, she actually managed that situation relatively effectively and neither my brother nor I were ever denied anything and were able to attend the colleges of our choice. But my mother established a pattern of relying on her Minneapolis brother for financial advice. The bulk of my father's estate was invested in shares in his company. Over the years he had purchased those shares as a way of signifying his confidence in the organization. While they had appreciated around the time of his death, they were not income producing. My uncle felt that my mother needed to convert those shares into more conservative investments that would provide her with a regular income. I learned that advice was difficult for my mother to accept because she felt that she was betraying my father's memory and confidence in the company in which he worked. Over the subsequent years various members of my father's family reminded her that if she had kept those investments going she would have been a millionaire. But while difficult, my mother followed my uncle's advice about her financial situation. That led to a pattern of regular visits between Aberdeen and Minneapolis and what seemed to me evidence of my mother's lack of confidence in making financial decisions on her own. By that time, my uncle had remarried and lived comfortably off one of the lakes inside Minneapolis.

I don't know how much time my mother spent reflecting on her status as a widow. She may have focused on day-to-day activities and thus avoided thinking about the broader situation. She did have friends and took responsibility for organizing a number of community activities, most of which centered on ways to make the broader community sensitive to the issues faced by the new state of Israel. Neither she or my brother and I ever referred to the promise she had made to us the day of my father's funeral that she would not remarry or move away from Aberdeen.

Years later when I started visiting India, I recognized that the problems that widows faced in India were not that different from those experienced by my mother. While the Indian communities had devised extreme rituals like sati (where the widow was expected to throw herself on her husband's funeral pyre), both cultures did not create a real place for the widow in the society. While the small Jewish community was supportive, my mother was a square peg in a round hole. She never learned to drive and was always dependent on others for moving around the community when a journey required more than a few blocks walk from our house.

MOTHER'S ILLNESS

While I didn't think of my mother as a sickly person, it became clear around the time I went to college that she had some significant health issues. And when my brother left for college two years later, there seemed to be a relationship between the empty nest syndrome and her health problems. Our long time family doctor found that she had arterial sclerosis and needed to be attentive to her eating patterns and general health habits. She was careful of her diet and took her medications seriously. Despite this, when it was time for me to graduate from college, her doctor didn't want her to travel for the occasion. Instead, my father's sister, Rose, was deputized to come to Ohio for the event. I know that my mother was not happy about this substitution but I was focused on my next steps and wasn't particularly attentive to her response to the circumstances.

Her health continued to deteriorate and in the next five or so years it became obvious that she would not be able to manage on her own. The decision about her next steps really did not involve either my brother or me. Instead, the person who made the decision (and who had been more attentive to her needs than her children) was her brother in Minneapolis. My mother was moved to the Jewish Home in St. Paul – the very institution where her father had died.

My brother and I were given responsibility for closing my mother's home. Although she was still alive, the process of going through her possessions effectively closed a chapter for both of us. We weren't surprised that she had organized her possessions carefully; most of them were labeled and we were not required to unwrap the boxes and envelopes because she had already told us in attached notes what was in their contents. As we sorted through her treasures we tried to determine who would get what and what items should be sold or given away. I was more likely to vote for keeping things, putting them in storage and then going through them leisurely when I had space for those contents. There were two types of items that we both wanted to claim. One type involved kitchen pots and pans (particularly heavy frying pans and pots that evoked strong and familiar memories). The other involved her rugs – Oriental rugs that she had from her days in the carpet business in New York City and a few American Indian rugs that my mother had collected over the years.

But the most poignant moment in the closing up process involved the dining room set (table, chairs, hutch) and the bedroom set (bed, side tables, and several chests of drawers). Both of these sets were in the New England style and crafted out of maple wood. We knew that these sets had been a part of our entire lives and were substantial pieces of furniture. We decided to contact the local furniture store to see if they were interested in purchasing the items or would suggest a way of disposing them. The response to the telephone call to the owner of the furniture store really surprised us. It turned out that the owner had sold the furniture to my parents in the first months of opening the store. Not only was it the major purchase that my parents had made when they moved into their rented house but it was the first major sale that the owner had made. It seemed that he had treasured that memory. When he heard that we wanted to sell the furniture, he told us that he wanted to buy it for one of his children who had recently moved into a new house. It seemed appropriate that those items stay in Aberdeen even though our family would not be there.

For the next few years my brother and I (and his wife and daughter) made occasional visits to St. Paul to see my mother at the Jewish Home. As time elapsed she became weaker and weaker until she was put on life support systems. My brother and I were there when the doctors told us that the risk of infection from the system was very strong and they recommended that my mother be taken off the system. Neither my brother nor I were comfortable with that recommendation and our guilt about the lack of our involvement in her care made it very hard for us to accept it. Following the pattern of the past, our role in the situation faded and my uncle made the decision to accept the doctors' recommendation. Ironically, stopping the life support system did not stop my mother. I believe that she lived for approximately six months after the decision to turn off the life support was made.

When my mother eventually died her burial and mourning process took place in the home of my uncle and his wife in Minneapolis. Although the shiva process continued through the traditional week of mourning, there were very few people who came to the house. Indeed, since neither my brother nor I had ties in Minneapolis, most of the individuals who came were distant relatives and friends of my uncle's and his family. The night before the funeral the rabbi who would preside over the service came to learn something about my mother's life. I do not think that any of those present made reference to the life she had in New York City before her marriage. There were occasional glimpses of her community activities and my acknowledgement that she had always been concerned about issues regarding women and that our library had books about that subject.

I did tell the gathered group about my experience in graduate school when I told my mother that I was taking a course with sociologist Arnold Rose on the U.S. Jewish community. I had decided to write a paper on the effect of the creation of the state of Israel on the American Jewish community and in a rare case of reaching out to my mother about my academic work, wrote a note to her about that assignment. Within a week I received a four or five page memo from her that was an annotated bibliography on the topic based on books in our house that she analyzed to help me. That was one of the few glimpses I had of her abilities that moved beyond her traditional role as a wife and a mother. But her funeral – unlike the others that preceded hers – marked a time when I was no longer an observer of death but someone who had to acknowledge its existence. I was relatively young to have lost both parents; I was thirty-six when my mother died.

LIVING WITH HEALTH ISSUES AND DEATH

In the years that followed there were a number of health problems and deaths of family members. I realized around my late fifties that few of my aunts and uncles were still alive. Too frequently family meetings took place during funerals or, if lucky, at an opportunity to say goodbye before someone had died. Luckily I had developed close relationships with a number of my cousins and thus had the sense of continuity within the family. When I reached the age of seventy-two, I realized that was the age when my mother had died. My brother had a similar realization when he reached the age of my father's death.

As I reached my seventies, I began to experience deaths of close friends. The first of these deaths was very unexpected. Eden Lipson, a long time friend (dating from my Berkeley days) who was on the New York Times Book Review staff had pancreatic cancer and was able to live several years after her diagnosis. She was quite young and her death was very hard for me to absorb. I watched how she was able to die gracefully and make the most of the time that was available. Several years later, Carla Cohen, my closest friend in Washington (a colleague from Antioch days) was diagnosed with bile duct cancer and lived for about six months. Given the long life of her mother (her mother lived to be over one hundred) she did not expect to deal with death at her age. By contrast, I found it surprising when I surpassed my mother's age. She, like Eden, was able to confront her death, say goodbye to family and close friends, and celebrate her career and family accomplishments. And her husband – also a long time close friend – died a few years later.

I do not know whether others had the experience of living with these difficult issues related to life and death. As my life developed, I was aware at some level of consciousness of the frailty of the future. I'm sure that played an important role in the way that I thought about my life. But as the time gets closer, the very task of writing this memoir allows me to absorb some elements of my earlier experiences.

PART II
Leaving Home

CHAPTER 5
Antioch College

I think that I started thinking seriously about where I would apply for college during my junior year in high school. My familiarity with Madison, Wisconsin and the presence of family in Wisconsin made it seem inevitable that I would apply to the University of Wisconsin. But that wasn't the place I wanted to attend. Before she became sick, my Aunt Miriam had told me about a college – Antioch College – that she thought would attract me. She had tried to interest her daughter in it but it didn't resonate with her. My mother hadn't ever heard of that school and when I obtained information about it, it didn't seem to her like a traditional institution of higher education. She did check with one of the few people in Aberdeen who she thought might be familiar with it. One of the Jewish families in town had two sons who had been students at the University of Chicago's Hutchins Program and were familiar with nontraditional liberal arts education. The Hutchins Program admitted students who would normally be in their junior year in high school and devised a program that allowed them to complete high school and obtain a BA degree within four years. When my mother checked with the younger son about the school, he was very positive about my Aunt Miriam's suggestion. Thus the combination of the two recommendations made that program seem like a possibility.

When I read the catalogue issued by Antioch College in Yellow Springs, Ohio I thought that program was designed especially for me. I recently was given a copy of that document (issued in the early 1950s). Rereading it after many years reinforced my view that something presented in a relatively traditional written form can dramatically communicate an educational vision. These elements don't seem so dramatic today but they were revolutionary in the mid 1950s. The elements that I remember exciting me included the small size of the student body, small classes with extensive contact between faculty and students, a liberal arts curriculum that provided opportunities for students to waive requirements, a co-ed student body, a governance system that allowed students to participate in decision-making, and what is called the "co-op" program – opportunities for students to alternate time on the campus with relevant jobs found all over the country. Although the total student body at the time was around 1,000, only about half of the students were on campus at one time because of the co-op program.

When I thought about college I wasn't thinking about educational opportunities for women, but I soon learned that Antioch had a special sensitivity to provide women a comfortable setting that offered them opportunities to learn. (Many years later I discovered a book entitled *Women's Ways of Knowing* by Mary Field Belenky and her associates that described an effective approach toward education for women that turned out to be found at Antioch.)

At that point I didn't know anything about John Dewey's theories of education but I learned that Antioch clearly had adopted his pragmatic belief that one could combine theory and practice in an educational setting. Once I arrived on campus I also learned that Antioch had been founded by Horace Mann, the father of universal public education and that it was linked to a hundred years of social change (it was the first private school to admit students of color). And to top it off, I learned that Arthur Morgan, the father of the New Deal Tennessee Valley Authority (TVA), had been the president of the college and conceived the co-op program.

To satisfy family members I applied both to Antioch and the University of Wisconsin. When I was admitted to Antioch, I made it clear that it was my real choice. I did not think that I needed to visit the campus because that magic catalogue had done its job. Because the college was unfamiliar to so many people, I created an explanation for my choice. I told people that I was looking for some place that was far from Aberdeen. When I considered the alternatives in alphabetical order, I thought that Alaska was too far away. But Antioch in Ohio seemed just fine.

Because Antioch had a somewhat different academic calendar than most other places, I was the first person in my high school class to leave for college. A group of my friends came to say goodbye at the Aberdeen train station even though the train left Aberdeen around one a.m. I took the train to Chicago and then changed trains to Xenia, Ohio, the closest train station to Yellow Springs. The train from Chicago to Xenia seemed to be a throwback to transportation earlier in the century. Indeed, it had potbelly stoves in the middle of the coaches to provide heat during the winter. But I remember feeling excited about the trip and departed Aberdeen with a sense of freedom.

I was met at the train by an upperclassman who helped me collect the belongings that I brought with me on the train. Those were the days when most belongings were sent to campus separately in a trunk. The minute we arrived on campus I felt I belonged there. The campus was situated just off Glen Helen, a 1,000-acre nature preserve of woods, waterways, prairies, and fields. The campus itself contained a number of buildings that dated back to the 19th century. The visual design of the campus ranged from the Main Building (designed in the style of James Renwick, the architect of the original building of the Smithsonian Institution) to Birch Hall, a building designed by architect Aero Saarinen and built only a few years before I arrived. At the time, both the library and the student center were still modest wooden buildings.

I was escorted to my dormitory, a building called North Hall that was built about the same time as the Main Building. It seemed to be in the middle of everything that occurred on campus, particularly weekly folk dances on the red brick area (called Red Square) in front of the building. Each floor of the building had two separate areas. Each had a name and upperclass women who were assigned to serve as the counselors for the students in their section. Gender segregation within the dorms was the rule of the day. When I found my room, the person who was assigned as my roommate wasn't there but it looked as if she had already moved in.

The room seemed simple but perfectly acceptable to me.

After unpacking, one of my first acts was to walk up and down the halls not only of my floor but others as well and look at the names of the individuals assigned to the rooms. One of my classmates later told me that she was watching me and was surprised to learn that I was actually counting the names of people with Jewish last names. In some primitive way – and probably not anticipating this – I found it very reassuring to be in an environment surrounded by other Jews. Those classmates were most often from the urban east coast (such as the New York City environs, New Jersey and Philadelphia).

When I met my roommate, I discovered another interesting pattern that illustrated an Antioch approach. My roommate was a young woman who had grown up in Kentucky. She was a very light skinned African American whose father had a funeral parlor located at the border of the African American and white sections of their town. A few years earlier, her mother had died and her father decided to send her to boarding school on the west coast. That boarding school was not desegregated but evidently no one thought of her as "colored." That was a very uncomfortable situation for her and somehow her father (who knew one of the music faculty members at Antioch) arranged for her to spend her last year in high school in Yellow Springs and then to attend Antioch College.

I was intrigued by the decision of Antioch staffers to put the two of us together. In some ways we were very different people with dramatically different backgrounds. But in other ways, we shared some experiences. We were both from non-urban environments but both of us had lived or travelled to other areas. Both of us had lost a parent at an early age. And both of us didn't fit the stereotypes of our backgrounds; in effect, both of us could "pass." While we had different interests, I felt close to her because her family friend on the faculty turned out to be the music faculty member with whom I eventually studied.

ACADEMICS

Perhaps my experience in the progressive elements of the Aberdeen school system had prepared me for Antioch. But whatever the reason, I clearly thrived. One of my earliest assignments in American history (the field that became my major) was to research Eleanor Roosevelt's role in the period between the first election of Franklin D. Roosevelt and when he assumed office. At that point, there were four months between those events and the effects of the depression of the time called for at least symbolic action by the couple that would assume the White House. I sat in the library reading the microfilms of the *New York Times* and other newspapers published during that period. I read the statements that Mrs. Roosevelt was making to an American public that was clearly depressed about the future and upset by the economic conditions of the time. She regularly provided low cost, high nutritional menus for the public in the newspapers, offering them a small boost of possibility for change. I sat at the library, rolling the microfilms, and crying at the same time because I was so moved by Mrs. Roosevelt's ability to empathize with the newspaper readers. My reaction was not viewed as strange in the Antioch environment.

I took required science courses that were structured in a way that was comfortable for a non-science major. One course was called Physical Science for the Consumer and taught students (among other things) how to wire an electrical socket and change oil in a car. One of my favorite courses was an offering in history entitled Western Civilization, a course based on one created at Columbia University that gave students the assignment of determining through analysis of original documents what actually happened to Louis the XIV after the French Revolution started. At that point I learned that history wasn't simply memorizing dates and battles but thinking about the role of actual human beings in the development of important changes. When I was in a Russian history course I carried around a copy of *Three Who Made a Revolution* by Bertram Wolfe, an incredibly riveting account of the Russian revolution. I was so attached to that book that some of my friends started saying that I envisioned being in that environment and saw myself as the fourth of those who made a revolution.

Life at Antioch really previewed the cultures of the 1960s. Folk music records blared from the dormitory rooms and performers such as Pete Seeger made almost annual visits to the campus during a time when he wasn't welcome in many more mainstream places. We were conscious of civil rights issues, many of which were illustrated by problems in southern Ohio.

During my last year on campus I took a course on 20th century American history that had been funded by a foundation to test different teaching methods. Students were given a test on the substance of the course at the beginning of the term. At that point, the teacher provided a syllabus and told us that we were responsible for organizing the specific class meetings and the discussions that would follow. Specific assignments were provided by the teacher and we were given the opportunity to invite him to be a guest lecturer for a limited number of sessions. The class was small – I think about ten people – and everyone in it was challenged by this experiment. We not only had good conversations during class but inevitably continued them at the lunch time that followed. At the end of the term, we were given the same test that we had taken at the beginning of the class. The results indicated that we had absorbed a lot of information during that period and seemed to show that students could be challenged by self-organized learning. I never learned if other faculty tried the same approach and experimented with that design.

In addition to my academic focus that balanced required courses with courses in my major (history), I spent a lot of time and energy in the music department on campus. The chair of the department was the only African American faculty member at the time and he was a very talented musician who was familiar with a wide range of musical approaches. He became my music mentor, continuing my classical music piano lessons from Aberdeen, and brought spirituals and traditional African American music to the student body. He introduced me to a range of two piano pieces, some involving two people playing on separate pianos (called four hand pieces) and others involving four people, two on each piano (called eight hands). I was joined in the eight hand efforts by the faculty member and two other students in performances of Brahms' Hungarian Dances, an experience of collaborative activity that I found energizing and beautiful.

FRIENDSHIPS AND ACTIVITIES

It was common that friendships that were developed both on campus and during coop jobs turned out to be very long lasting. Each academic and job experience provided opportunities for students to share their views and comment on the ideas that they were exposed to. That exchange occurred throughout the campus in almost any location that provided space for discussion. Many of the friendships that I developed both on campus and during my co-op jobs have continued through the years.

One of my favorite locations on campus was in the campus Tea Room. In addition to the traditional cafeteria meals, students could use their meal tickets to eat in the campus Tea Room, an establishment in an old house that allowed students to order from a menu. Like everything else at Antioch, that process involved the student in somewhat untraditional ways. Each person filled out the individual order slip with his or her food choice and signed a name to the order. Rarely was that name the actual name of the student. During my last year on campus when I was enrolled in the 20th century American history course I decided to use the name of Ida Tarbell, an important muckraker journalist in the early years of the 20th century. My sense of identity with Tarbell grew during those months and my friends goaded me on with that identity. When two of those friends were married a year later, I couldn't attend the wedding but happily sent a congratulatory telegram signed by Ida Tarbell.

Although this was an era that previewed the 1960s world of civil rights and anti-war demonstrations, Antioch seemed to anticipate that set of developments. During my last year on campus there was a conflict between the views of a new college president and the "norms" of the campus. Not surprisingly, the issues in conflict involved a dress code. The president decided that no one would be allowed in the student cafeteria without shoes. Although student dress on campus was extremely informal (the common uniform worn by both sexes was blue jeans and sweatshirts), many students felt that it was both appropriate to arrive at the cafeteria without shoes and – as a matter of principle – to believe that it was the individual student's choice of what footwear to use or not. Students usually owned two sets of clothing – one that they wore on campus and one that they wore on their co-op job where they sought to blend into a regular staff.

The demonstration that was organized to support the no-shoes stance was quite creative and meant to illustrate the ridiculousness of the requirement. A Victorian tea party was scheduled on the large lawn in front of the Main Hall. Students were told to dress up for the event. That meant that women were encouraged to wear hats and gloves (the hats were obtained from the costume supply in the closets of the drama department) and men were told to wear suits and formal wear. Music was supplied by a student violinist who had parted his hair in the middle, slicked it down with goop, and came out looking like a classic Victorian musician. Tea and small snacks were served. We didn't win that battle but it was an absolutely delightful afternoon.

The speaker at my Antioch graduation in 1958 exemplified the values that were being emphasized in the college. Linus Pauling had received the Nobel Prize in Chemistry in 1954 and was a very public scientist teaching at Cal Tech. In addition to his scientific work, he was a peace activist who worked closely with the Quaker group, the American Friends Service Committee. His commencement address was entitled "The Place of Science in the Modern World" and I remember him emphasizing his remarks by pulling out a model of a molecular structure from a green book bag. I think that structure was related to his research on Vitamin C and his belief that supplemental amounts of the substance would be effective in warding off colds and other illnesses. His presentation (and his life) gave the graduating class a model of personal and academic possibilities.

THEORY AND PRACTICE

It seemed that Dewey's advice about the importance of linking theory and practice permeated everything at Antioch. I read a lot of Dewey in my years at Antioch since the senior Antioch philosophy professor was Dewey's last doctoral student. But it was not only Dewey's writings that influenced me. My long-term commitment to the interrelationship between theory and practice probably came from the structure of the co-op program.

I had spent my entire freshman year on campus but looked forward to the work opportunities that might be available to me in succeeding years. I was planning to graduate in four years rather than five (possible because I was able to waive a number of courses through examinations) and thus I looked forward to three different work experiences. The term "work" was defined very broadly. It not only included the tasks of a job but also gave the student the opportunity to live and work in a new and often strange environment. It was quite common for a student from an east coast urban area to find a job in a less urban Midwestern or western city. I had spent one summer back in Aberdeen working for the Probation Office in the County Court House. I saw another aspect of that community when I met with juveniles from rural areas outside of town who had been arrested, often for crimes that reflected their sense of isolation from the rest of the world.

In my case, my first co-op job was located in Washington, D.C. at The Associated Press. While it was fascinating for me to be in the AP environment, it was even more fascinating to be living in D.C. Two of my Antioch colleagues and I found an apartment in the Adams-Morgan area on Kalorama Street, explored all aspects of the city, and made the Phillips Art Gallery's concert series our regular destination. Our apartment was in a converted brownstone and I was introduced to cockroaches and waterbugs for the first time. Both the AP job and the apartment had been utilized by earlier Antioch students and so the grapevine provided us with a relatively easy transition to the city. The structure of the co-op program varied. But in this instance I spent the first few months of the academic year on campus, the next few months in Washington, the next months on campus, and the last months back in D.C.

By the beginning of my third year at Antioch, I decided that I wanted to take a job in the structure of the campus government. Antioch had two decision-making bodies: an administrative council (faculty, administrators, and a few students) and a community council (largely controlled by students). The staff of the community council was modeled on the city manager format – a professional staff responsible for running the activities of the council as well as staffing its regular meetings. Thus a full time Community Manager and a full time Assistant Community Manager (both of whom were students) were chosen each year. My job was the Assistant Community Manager position and gave me an opportunity to work closely with the Manager (who was a friend) and to have my first introduction to the business of government.

As I reflect on that experience, it probably was more influential than I thought at the time. I enjoyed being in an environment that involved collegial decision-making and sought to deal with issues that had a varied constituency. Antioch students were hardly monolithic and they represented many different perspectives on day-to-day campus issues. And the job also gave me an opportunity to live off campus in Yellow Springs and experience another aspect of that community, particularly the few shops and restaurants on the main street.

My last co-op job was in New York City working in the United Nations press office. My academic work exposed me to international issues and I was intrigued by the possibility of living in Manhattan. I had visited New York City during vacations and had some sense of the many possibilities there. I remember standing on the street at the 42nd Street Library for the first time, thinking about the novels I had read that gave me a familiarity with the scene. Interestingly enough, I totally failed to think about my mother's decade of life in the city but sought to establish my own memories of the place. As I was visiting one of the city's many museums, I bumped into my brother who – unbeknownst to me – was visiting the city (he was also an Antioch student).

My roommate and I had a basement apartment on the upper west side within walking distance of Columbia University and a half a block off Broadway. It was convenient for us to get around the city with easy access to the subway and buses. The apartment was somewhat strange in structure; the bathtub was in the kitchen and the very large wood paneled living room also doubled as a second bedroom. We believed that we had trained the resident cockroaches to hide when we turned on a light and thus devised a ritual of flipping the light switch a few minutes before we wanted to enter the room.

Both our neighborhood and the UN itself were incredibly cosmopolitan. One never knew what language would be spoken around you or who your neighbors might be. The diversity of the UN staff made day-to-day life very interesting. It was a great place for me to celebrate my 21st birthday. One of the officials in the press office was an official from India who had a map of the world on his wall. That was unlike any other map I had ever seen; the center of the map was India and the rest of the world was placed around it. Years later, after I spent quite a lot of time in India, I realize that indeed many of its citizens thought that India was at the center of the world. But my favorite UN story was about a telephone exchange between two staff members who were involved in the same project. Both were not very communicative and were quite terse in their exchange. The first called and identified himself: "Katz here." The second responded, "Katz, Miao." The latter was pronounced, "meow." Sometimes the policy exchanges between countries didn't get much more substantive than that.

Each of my co-op assignments had a substantive impact on my personal development that went beyond preparation for entering the workforce as an adult. In fact, after I left Antioch I continued the pattern that I had devised to try out jobs and locations. It took many years before I had a job that lasted more than two years. I guess I was still in the pattern of experimenting with elements in a career.

DEFINING JUDAISM

My first day at Antioch noting the presence of Jewish classmates illustrated that I found it quite reassuring to be in an environment where it wasn't strange to be Jewish. While that was something I appreciated, I was not very clear about what it meant to be Jewish. Some elements of my discomfort with the Jewish community in Aberdeen continued. And there were also some attributes and values expressed by some members of my extended family that did not make me comfortable.

Although the percent of students with Jewish backgrounds at Antioch was quite significant, there was no formal acknowledgement of that. The campus was highly secular and openness to new ideas was perhaps the closest thing to a religious belief within the community. But there was one exception: a Quaker meetinghouse on the fringe of the campus that held Sunday meetings every week.

It is still not clear to me why I began attending those meetings. Perhaps I needed a break in my schedule and an opportunity to reflect on what had happened during the week. That reflection was personal and almost always silent. Perhaps I was shopping for some religious identity that would be an alternative to traditional Judaism. Or perhaps I liked the idea that there was not a formal hierarchy in those meetings. For whatever reason, I found it very satisfying to attend those meetings when I was on campus. I found the tradition of gathering in silence without the services of a designated leader to be a good way to end a week and think about the coming week.

The regular attendees at the Yellow Springs Quaker meeting were often faculty from the college and their families. Although a few of them were birthright Quakers (born to a Quaker family, not converted to Quakerism), others were individuals who had been attracted to the form of worship. While students were in attendance, they were clearly the minority. The individuals who spoke (when the spirit moved them) were more likely to be from the settled community, not from the student population. It was interesting to hear what was on their minds and it seemed to me to provide a way to erase the dividing line between faculty and students.

At the same time, when it was possible I did attend High Holiday services held in synagogues in Columbus or other cities in the region. I realized neither my background nor my personality fit the quiet, silent mood of a Quaker meeting. I was uncomfortable with the silence of the meeting. I was – and continue to be – an outspoken individual who is often the first person in a meeting to speak and who is likely to try to convince others of my views. So given my personality I wasn't likely to make Quakerism a permanent identity.

During my last year on campus there was an interesting test of my definition of Judaism. A student from the Reform rabbinical college in Cincinnati came to Antioch to try to convince students on campus that a Hillel program should be established at Antioch. He was someone who had considered attending Antioch as an undergraduate but had decided to move in a different direction and was now studying to become a rabbi. His commitment to Jewish identity was very strong and he was convinced that the Antioch student body represented a fertile field for his efforts to develop stronger Jewish identity in nontraditional academic programs. His view of Judaism was not a traditional one and he was comfortable with people and ideas that were not usually found in the organized Jewish community.

Evidently someone had suggested that he meet with some students and I found myself sitting around a table in the coffee shop with a few other students. He was very earnest and tried hard to understand why this group of students – who clearly identified as Jews – were very skeptical about creating a Hillel on campus. I'm not sure that any of us could explain our perspective very effectively but it was clear that each person in that group was searching for a way to identify as a Jew in nontraditional ways. That might have started with skepticism about establishing a Hillel on campus but was also likely to move to discomfort about joining traditional synagogues or traditional Jewish organizations.

It is interesting that this rabbinical student finished the Reform seminary and eventually took a job as a rabbi in a synagogue in Columbia, Maryland (one of the new towns established in the 1960s). When he retired (nearly forty years after our meeting at Antioch), the newspaper covering his retirement described him as someone who is "unaffiliated with any branch of Judaism, welcomes Zen Buddhists and Jews for Jesus alongside Orthodox and Reform members." He seemed to have found a way to live with the kind of multiple identities that were behind the skepticism of the Antioch students.

While I was skeptical about bringing a traditional approach to Judaism to Antioch, I continued to find ways to maintain my identification as a Jew during those years. And I welcomed the packages of goodies that my mother sent me to mark other Jewish holidays.

AFTER ANTIOCH

I completed my four years at Antioch with some attributes that developed more fully over the next fifty years. But I was also unformed in many other ways. I was interested in politics, in ideas, and concerned about social change. As one friend remembers, I was the person who when asked, "How are you?" (a perfunctory question), usually told the questioner in some detail how I was. I hadn't learned how to respond to those kind of superficial queries. Yet in other ways (particularly in terms of career development) I was more likely to be able to tell you what I didn't want to do rather than what I would like to do.

I did realize this inchoate side of myself and decided that the best thing for me to do was to continue school. Despite my personal commitment to find ways to link theory and practice, it seemed rational to continue my education. A conversation with one of my faculty advisors contributed to my decision to apply (and be accepted) to a master's degree program in American Studies at the University of Minnesota in the Twin Cities. I had no idea what I might do with that degree and didn't seem to realize that this decision represented a return to the part of the Midwest that I escaped from. That year of graduate school was wonderful. I was surrounded by stimulating faculty and a set of colleagues who continued the intellectual journey that I had started at Antioch. When I completed that year, I realized that it was time to start a career. But that was a process that lasted for many years.

CHAPTER 6
Trains, Planes, and Travel

Sometime relatively early in my life I heard the phrase "wandering Jew." I had no idea where the term came from but it resonated with me. There was something about a people wandering the globe that appealed to me. I found myself cultivating the houseplant called "wandering Jew" without realizing that I was attracted to something that liked to move in new and often unpredictable directions.

When I was old enough to realize where the term came from, I learned it had a very different meaning than I had assumed. I think I was attracted to the phrase because, as early as I can remember, I knew that my place of residence wasn't the center of the universe and that I may have been destined to "wander." Perhaps this belief emerged because my extended family did not live close by. Visits to them usually required a train or car ride (to both Minneapolis/St. Paul and Milwaukee) and a realization that their life was quite different from mine. When I was old enough to learn about the diaspora that occurred after the destruction of the First Temple in Jerusalem in the 6th century BCE, I began to understand why Jews were found across the globe.

But my sense of wandering started with train journeys that began in Aberdeen. The train station in Aberdeen was in the geographic center of the town and it was clear that many social and economic transactions emerged from that station. But I knew that the train station was not the end point or the center of my universe; rather, it was the first leg to another place. The earliest ritual that I remember involved getting on the local train to Minneapolis in the early evening, dressed in pajamas and ready to find the sleeper car and the berth that we would occupy. Although some trains had compartments, the sleeper car was a series of upper and lower berths that could be turned into seats in the morning. The travelers were usually my mother, brother and me and we had reserved two berths (the upper and lower) that required one of the children to share a berth with my mother. I loved the ritual of finding the berth, meeting the porter, and getting ready to go to sleep. The berth itself had a number of mesh containers that allowed you to store your treasures yet see them through the mesh. The train (called a milk train because it stopped at so many places along the route to pick up and deliver milk) progressed leisurely along the 200 miles from Aberdeen to Minneapolis. It arrived in Minneapolis around six a.m. but we usually did not disembark until somewhat later in the morning having replaced our pajamas with clothing for the day ahead.

Getting off the train was also a part of the adventure. We would say goodbye to the porter and then go into the station. That transition immediately let you know you were in an urban environment. I especially liked the return trip, which allowed us to sit in a large waiting room in either Minneapolis or Milwaukee and watch fellow passengers. I still have a strong memory of sitting in one of those waiting rooms decorated with huge photographic murals of western mountains that lined the train route through Montana and places further west.

The train station was always a place for surprises. One day we were waiting for the train in Minneapolis and all of a sudden a large group of Japanese people came into the waiting room. There were men, women and children in the group and they looked very uncomfortable as they found places to sit. It turned out that it was a group of Japanese who were being moved from the west coast as a part of the internment of Japanese people during World War II. My parents tried to provide explanations for why this group of people was taking the train but I could not comprehend why this was happening. I didn't understand why these people were not trusted by the U.S. government.

Train trips were a normal part of my life and thus it wasn't surprising that when I was about nine, my parents were comfortable allowing me to take the train alone to Milwaukee. Although the trip involved an overnight stay and most of another day, I knew what to do and the porter agreed to look after me. I don't remember being overwhelmed by the trip and followed the rituals that were familiar to me including meals in the dining car. My aunt collected me at the train station and, after a short visit in Milwaukee, we went on to Madison where I stayed with her for several weeks. That visit was the first time I was on my own (granted with a family member).

By the time I was in high school I expanded my travel routes to attend conferences and meetings. A B'nai Brith Youth Organization (BBYO) conference brought me to Chicago, which became my favorite train station for years. Like the city itself the train station was bustling and full of fascinating looking people. I knew about the organized crime population in Chicago and was convinced that many of the people I was watching had some connection to the Mafia. My four years at Antioch usually included train trips that went through Chicago. There were stories in the paper about murders where the bodies were placed in suitcases. I couldn't take my eyes off of the large suitcases that were all over the station since I was convinced they contained body parts. Some years later when I was visiting in Chicago, I picked up the newspaper and read about the murder of someone who had married a woman from Aberdeen probably twenty years earlier. A suitcase was delivered to this woman that contained her husband's body. My fantasy stories as a child weren't so far from reality.

By my last year of college an airport in Aberdeen provided another travel option. Flights were available from Aberdeen to Minneapolis/St. Paul and then further east. And when at Antioch I was more likely to go by car to take me places during holidays or when I went to my co-op job in New York or Washington, D.C. But planes never had the allure of trains, and as my travelling expanded I would search for opportunities to take the train. It wasn't always easy to find convenient train travel in the U.S., but I managed to have a train trip from the San Francisco area to Chicago that gave me a glimpse of parts of the U.S. I hadn't seen. While I might have arrived abroad via plane or ship, I often moved through a new country on the train. Despite the cultural differences between countries, there was always something familiar about train travel. Over the decades that involved trains in the United Kingdom, the USSR, Poland, Greece, France, Australia, India and China.

CROSSING THE BORDERS

As a result of my trips out of Aberdeen I had learned that each new location had its own idiosyncrasies and cultures. When I began to explore different parts of the world, those differences became extremely interesting and I tried to understand them. At the same time, I tried to combine those elements that were familiar with those that were new. Unlike many young people today, I didn't leave the shores of the U.S. until I was in my late twenties. My first trip abroad was to England and my journey there involved crossing the Atlantic on the *SS United States*. I embarked on the ship in New York City, found my cabin, and prepared for a luxurious journey. I remember watching the Statue of Liberty disappear from my sight as we made our way to the ocean. About the time that occurred, I found myself with a fairly severe case of seasickness. For the next three plus days, I stayed in my cabin. I wasn't ever sure whether I had a predilection for seasickness or whether the psychological pressures of beginning this adventure had captured me. By the time we disembarked, I seemed to be over that illness and was ready to get to London.

That trip to the UK started a pattern that I didn't develop consciously. From that time on, almost all of my trips abroad involved a dual agenda. While always interested in seeing the sights and experiencing the joys of tourism, I also have tried to find ways to enter the society I was visiting. That could be through some kind of work experience or professional associations or through ways to enter the day-to-day life of that new society through friends.

My experience in England contained all of these attributes. I had left a job at the U.S. Commission on Civil Rights in Washington, D.C. and decided to go to London to focus on immigration and civil rights issues. I planned to stay as long as my money lasted; that turned out to be nearly a year. A visitor to the Civil Rights Commission from the UK encouraged me to make that trip and provided me with contacts both for work and for housing. He became an important link to that new world. In that case, I went with the flow. I rented a room in the house of a very interesting and committed family and thus had the opportunity to get inside their world. I went to work nearly every day on the bus, shopped in the local markets, spent many Saturdays at the British Museum, took advantage of London theatre, and through my study assignment, journeyed across the UK to interview immigrant groups and trade union officials about the status of their relationships. I learned that people were willing to talk to an American who was interested in what they were doing.

My love of Indian food was generated by my visits across the UK where very good Pakistani or Indian restaurants were found in almost every city. I discovered some distant cousins whose life gave me a glimpse of the world of British intellectuals. Their household combined many of the elements that intrigued me: Jewish culture, left wing political discussion, and skepticism about the U.S. This household became the subject of a recent and fascinating book written by their grandson, Sasha Abramski, *The House of Twenty Thousand Books*.

COMBINING WORK AND TOURISM

The pattern that I established in London became the template for subsequent visits outside of the U.S. I didn't like being a voyeur and thus the classic tourist structure didn't appeal to me. But I still wanted to see important sites and objects. Sometimes I found a way to embellish the tourist role by meeting people who suggested nontraditional ways of doing this. When I knew I would be in a country I tried to adjust my work travel schedule to allow me to organize events in places that I wanted to see. In other cases, I looked for work or professional opportunities in locations of interest. Either approach allowed me to move beyond the voyeur role. When my career was based in an academic setting, I had a number of different opportunities to attend conferences, use sabbaticals, and employ fellowships to experience different settings. I am writing this just a year after spending nearly a month in Hong Kong teaching at Hong Kong University. That time in Hong Kong gave me an unusual perspective to observe the way that society is struggling to find a way to maintain its values and history within the broader Chinese system.

Of my multiple global wanderings, several of them best illustrate the pattern of combining professional activities with exploration of new settings. A sabbatical allowed me to spend approximately five months in Australia in the Public Policy Program at the Australian National University in Canberra. I was a part of a newly minted graduate program and was involved in teaching and some research efforts. In addition to those responsibilities I knew that I wanted to see many places in the expansive country. I was able to rent an apartment and feel that I had moved into the day-to-day life in Canberra.

It was interesting how small things helped me understand the Australian culture. The Public Policy Program celebrated birthdays every month by purchasing a cake that would be shared by the faculty and staff at teatime. I noticed that the cake was always cut in absolutely equal pieces and distributed to everyone present. I realized that most U.S. settings would have approached that cake differently. A slice would be cut for each person who had the ability to say whether they wanted a small piece, a medium piece, or a large piece. In other words, each individual had the opportunity to request a specific order. To me the Australian approach reflected the strong egalitarian culture in that society. By contrast, the American approach emphasized individualism. I don't think I would have understood those differences if I had been a traditional tourist.

I have described my strategy in Australia as one of agreeing to speak on anything as long as the sponsor came up with an airplane ticket. I managed to visit much of Australia with that strategy, particularly aboriginal areas such as Alice Springs and Darwin in addition to the cities along the eastern and southern coasts. I was struck by the similarity between the aboriginal Australian communities and American Indian reservations in the Southwest.

That first visit to Australia led to many additional visits. Some of them involved research efforts, teaching, or conference presentations and all of them generated a host of close friends with whom I keep in contact. I continue to find it very comfortable to be in Australia and to follow the developments in that country. And Australia is a very easy place for Americans to "fit in" while it is different enough to be interesting.

My Fulbright in India also led to significant relationships. My preference for English-speaking societies and my fascination with the BBC series, *The Jewel in the Crown*, led me to apply for a grant in that country. When I knew I was likely to be approved for a Fulbright grant, I tried to learn a lot about that country and its political and bureaucratic institutions. At the same time, I found that novels written in English gave me a sense of that society. In addition, I took a course on Indian Art and Architecture at the Smithsonian Institution, which familiarized me with a number of significant sites within that country. My Fulbright was a three-month assignment; I was located in Delhi for two of the months and travelled around the country making presentations and visiting various organizations for the third month. A wonderful staff person at the USIA office in Delhi (who has become a close friend who created an organization for women in corporate India) was able to arrange for me to make presentations in relevant settings in locations that were near the sites that I wanted to visit. While I visited places that are well known (such as Sanchi and Jaipur), I also spent time in the south of India and one day was probably the only westerner in the tourist area of Kanyakumari, the southern most tip of India.

The institutional sponsor of my Fulbright was the Indian Institute of Public Administration located in Delhi. My responsibilities involved some teaching but also opportunities to meet with bureaucrats attending training sessions there and the faculty of the Institute. The contacts I made with those individuals were very useful when it was time for me to move out of Delhi. It certainly gave me a perspective on the day-to-day life of members of the Indian Administrative Service. This was reinforced by my weeklong visit to Mussoori, the training institute for public servants in the beautiful foothills of the Himalayas.

It turned out that I was the first American who was given a Fulbright placement in the Indian Institute of Public Administration. There had been resistance within the faculty to accept American scholars largely because of the belief among Indian intellectuals that most

Americans in India were actually CIA agents. It seemed that my Indian colleagues were convinced I was not a CIA spy when my description of developments in the U.S. emphasized the problems within the American society. That didn't seem to be the way that they thought CIA people would present a picture of the U.S.

When I learned that my Fulbright had been finalized and that I would be in Delhi during the very hot summer, I realized that I needed to find a place to live that would be comfortable in that climate. I placed an ad in the U.S. Embassy staff newsletter suggesting that there might be someone on the staff who might like to swap houses for several months. It turned out that a couple wanted to be in Washington for the birth of their baby during that period, so we swapped houses. They had my modest three-bedroom house in northwest D.C. and I had their elegant diplomatic house in a lovely neighborhood in Delhi. In addition, I had their staff – a cook, a maid, and part time gardener and laundry people. I also had responsibility for their nine-month-old golden retriever. The dog was convinced that he ruled the household and believed that any human being there was responsible for amusing him. While I enjoyed having him around, I sometimes had to hide from him if I had work to do. That sparked episodes where he would cry when he was alone. Although my perch in upscale Delhi wasn't a typical Indian dwelling, my interaction with the staff gave me another perspective on the country. And the cook was willing to give me recipes for the dishes that he had made for me.

The combination of day-to-day experiences, my contacts in the bureaucracy, and meeting other individuals in both social change settings and academic organizations provided me with a wonderful experience in India. I continued my interest in the country and returned there mostly for research and other academic reasons. And the individuals I have met have given me a rich view of that amazingly complex society.

JEWS FROM STRANGE PLACES

It was always clear to me that being Jewish and having roots in South Dakota was like an oxymoron – a case in contradictions. When I left for college I sought situations and experiences that seemed to reinforce the Jewish part of my identity. But I wasn't always comfortable with the experience of friends and acquaintances who had grown up in shtetl-like Jewish communities and who assumed that a clear cultural pattern was present in every other setting identified as "Jewish." When I started to travel around the globe, I usually tried to visit Jewish communities in various countries. While in London I went to a delicatessen in the East End. While the accent was different, the substance of the conversations was very familiar since many of the restaurant patrons were in similar occupations to Jewish communities in New York's lower east side. Wandering around that neighborhood I discovered a small bakery and started going there on Friday afternoons to buy bread. My conversations with the owner of the bakery led to an unusual account of her situation during World War II. It seemed that she had relatives in New York City who were very poor so she found ways to send food from her shop to them during the war – somewhat of a reverse of the American view of sending bundles to Britain.

Trips through Europe often involved stops at synagogues or other parts of Jewish communities in various cities. But my pattern of visits changed somewhat during a visit to the Soviet Union in the mid 1960s. This was a period still experiencing Cold War behaviors left over from the Stalinist era. I had joined a trip to the Soviet Union sponsored by the British National Union of Students. A friend in Washington had taken a similar trip a few years earlier and thought it was extremely interesting and very inexpensive. My role in London was close enough to that of a student to justify membership in that organization. The trip was by train, starting in London, crossing the channel, changing trains in Brest Litovsk, and arriving in what was then Leningrad (now St. Petersburg). We spent time there and then went on to Moscow and returned stopping in Warsaw. Before I had left the U.S. I had read Elie Wiesel's book, *The Jews of Silence*, an account of his trip to the Soviet Union. It made a great impression on me and I hoped that I would have a chance to observe the world that he described.

That trip evoked both familiar and unfamiliar reactions from me. Before arriving in Russia, the train had progressed through rural areas that were probably very similar to the areas where my parents were born. And the trip in March provided weather that was just like that in South Dakota – snow, cold, and over-heated temperatures when one went inside of buildings. I had read enough Turgenev and Tolstoy to envision Russian 19th century scenes. When we stopped in Brest Litovsk for five or six hours in the middle of the night to change trains, we found ourselves in a train station where men were playing cards and children in fur coats were running around – a scene that could have been straight from Turgenev.

Surprisingly, although the trip was sponsored by the British student group, almost all of the individuals in the group were either Americans or Canadians. I soon became friends with one of the other Americans, a law student from Chicago who had a yearlong fellowship in the UK. Besides turning into a good friend, he had a skill that was very useful: he spoke Russian. As a result we were able to have exchanges with people who were not necessarily a part of the formal visits.

There were many aspects of that trip that I will never forget. But it was our visit to the main synagogue in Moscow that was most meaningful. It was also the beginning of the *refusnik* movement when Jews in the Soviet Union were refused permission to emigrate, particularly to Israel. I was able to catch a glimpse of the anti-Semitism that Wiesel had described in his book.

We were walking along the streets in Moscow trying to find the synagogue. My friend went up to the police officer who was sitting in one of the tall traffic perches and asked him in Russian, "Where is the synagogue?" The officer looked at him and hearing an accent from an English speaker asked: "Don't they have synagogues in England?" Despite his comment, he did give us directions and we found the synagogue. It was a Saturday morning so the chief rabbi was around as were a number of congregants. I persuaded my friend to go up to the rabbi and ask him if he knew of my great-grandfather, Pincus Goldberg, the rabbi of Romanova. I was very surprised when he told us that he did indeed know of him and that he was someone who was admired. So much for my cynicism about the accuracy of stories of my mother's family!

As if that were not enough, when we left the synagogue we realized that we were being followed by someone who had been in the synagogue. He followed us for a few blocks and then felt comfortable starting a conversation. He was trying to leave the USSR to come to the U.S. and listened to Radio Free Europe on a regular basis. It was a poignant moment when we realized that there might be a significant emigration of Jews from the Soviet Union in coming years.

DISCOVERING REALLY STRANGE PLACES

While my Russian experience was powerful, it was not unfamiliar because mid 20th century Russian Jews shared many attributes with the earlier immigrants who had made their way to the U.S. (particularly food). But I had two other travel experiences that were quite dissimilar from my Jewish experience in South Dakota. Indeed, they made me appreciate the contemporary dimensions of the diaspora following the destruction of the First Temple in Jerusalem. While I thought that growing up Jewish in South Dakota was very unusual, it was nothing compared to the worlds that I discovered in India and Azerbaijan.

After about a month in Delhi on my Fulbright, I realized that there was a synagogue in an area near the Khan Market, an upscale shopping area in Delhi. I had been visiting temples and other religious sites around the city and thought it might be time for me to go to the local synagogue. I made arrangements for a taxi to take me to the Friday night service and to wait for me until the service was concluded. When I walked into the synagogue, I realized that I was the only westerner there. A woman in a sari came up to me and introduced herself. I learned that she and her husband had come to Delhi from Bombay (now Mumbai) soon after independence in 1947. Her husband was a bureaucrat in the then new government. She provided me with a few pamphlets on Jews in India that I promised to read after the service was concluded. We chatted and in the course of the conversation I asked her how long her family had been in India. I was stunned by her answer. She told me that her Jewish family had been in India for 2,000 years.

That simple answer to my question started me on an on-going quest for information about Jews in India. I learned that the woman in the synagogue was a member of the B'nai Israel community, a group of Jews who are thought to be descendants of people who were shipwrecked around 250 BC, stranded in an area of the state of Maharashtra (the state where Bombay is located) and unknown for centuries until they were discovered by a Catholic priest. I subsequently learned that there were at least two other Jewish communities in India – the Cochin community in the state of Kerala (dated to approximately 200 AD) and the Baghdadi community from Iraq (who arrived in the later part of the 19th century). Unlike the B'nai Israel community, the Cochin Jews were involved in trade and thus were known by Jewish communities in other parts of the world.

That visit to the Delhi synagogue spurred my interest and led to visits to B'nai Israel synagogues in Bombay and Ahmadabad and the still open Cochin synagogue that dated to the 16th century. To this day I am intrigued by the experience of Jews in India. I have learned about the possible existence of other Jewish communities in other parts of the country and saw how at least one of the communities was probably a part of the First Temple diaspora. Most of the Jews in India look very much like their Indian compatriots, either because of their years in other areas or because of intermarriage with local Indians. Yet at the same time, despite the absence of a Torah and other written information about observances, (as well as their isolation from other Jews), the B'nai Israel community managed to keep services and customs alive over the centuries through oral traditions. When some members of the community immigrated to Israel they maintained those ancient traditions.

The visit to the Bombay synagogue was incredibly moving for me. I arrived in Bombay on a Friday afternoon and telephoned someone from the United States Information Service (part of the State Department), who was a member of the B'nai Israel community. He was busy that evening but told me that I would be welcome to attend services at one of the B'nai Israel synagogues in the city. I took a taxi to the synagogue, which was located in a predominantly Moslem neighborhood. I arrived a few minutes before the service started and followed the classic Indian practice of removing my shoes before entering a place of worship.

I sat down in the area that was clearly demarcated for women and was given a prayer book. There were a number of people (mostly men) participating but many of the seats were empty. When the service started I found much of it unfamiliar. The service was led by an older man who was called "Reverend" (but was probably a rabbi). I expected to be an observer of the services and thus was surprised when I was called up to the bima (the raised platform where the rabbi led the service) and told that a special blessing would be said for me because "even though we didn't know who you were, we knew that you had come from a long distance to join us." I was incredibly touched.

After the service, the person in charge (known as the gabbai) asked me if I wanted to see their Torahs. He opened the ark, a beautiful wooden object that I learned had been constructed by members of the congregation who were skilled carpenters. But the most amazing things were the silver ornaments on the Torahs that were inside the ark. At that point in my stay in India I had learned something about tribal silver Indian jewelry – gorgeous pieces which had clearly influenced the Torah ornaments.

The gabbai told me that the synagogue often had trouble gathering enough congregants to make up the minyan – the ten men required to say some of the prayers. I had noticed that most of the individuals in the congregation were elderly; there were very few younger people. He told me, "The Jewish Agency stole all of our young people." In effect, he was telling me that many of the younger generation in the community had been convinced to emigrate to Israel. The same pattern was evident when I visited the synagogue in Ahmadabad although there was some evidence that younger members of the community who had emigrated to Israel had decided to return to India. Trips to Israel gave me an understanding of the disjuncture between the world that the B'nai Israel experienced in India and that of their new home in Israel. Indian Jews in Israel were likely to experience racial prejudice in Israel.

AZERBAIJAN

I discovered another pattern in the Jewish communities in Azerbaijan. There were two distinct Jewish communities in that Central Asian country in the Caucasus area, which bordered on the Caspian Sea. One involved the group called the "Mountain Jews" and the other individuals who had come to Azerbaijan from Russia. I was conducting a policy analysis workshop sponsored by a university in Baku, the capital of the country and, at the same time, visiting some friends who were living there. The friends I was visiting were also interested in learning about the Jewish community in that country; we had found some information about the Mountain Jews and they arranged a visit to the northeastern part of the country (a city called Quba which was the center of an important rug making area).

The Mountain Jews are usually described as the descendants of one of the ten lost Tribes and came to the mountainous area near Dagestan in Russia around the 5th century AD, moving north through Iran. Unlike other groups found in the countries of the area (Russians or Turks), their language (Tat) was thought to be derived from an ancient Persian source. Over the years they moved north into isolated areas to escape from conquering groups. Sometime (probably around the 18th century) the ruler of the city of Quba gave them land across the river from the main city to provide a refuge for them from various conquerors. Neighborhoods in that area were given the names of the villages from which the community members had escaped. That was the community we wanted to visit.

We left Baku early on a Friday afternoon, hoping to arrive in Quba before sundown in time to get to the synagogue. We were told that the synagogue was the only one still holding regular Friday night services although there were one or two other synagogues still operating in the area. We drove around the community before finding the synagogue, observing traditional Jewish symbols decorating many of the buildings. We arrived at the synagogue and were welcomed in. I don't remember what language was used to communicate with the synagogue officials. My friend spoke some Azeri but the community members were more likely to be comfortable with Russian and their Persian derived language.

I had two surprises when we entered the synagogue. The first was that women did not attend services and thus there wasn't a specified women's section that is usually found in a synagogue. We (one of my friends and I) were given special dispensation since we weren't a part of the community and were seated at the back. The man in our trio was just fine and sat in the midst of the regular male congregants. The second surprise involved the beauty of the synagogue. The floor of the synagogue was adorned with wonderful Azeri carpets. It looked more like a mosque than a traditional synagogue even though the physical structure of the ark and the bima were very familiar.

The service itself was actually more familiar to me than the Indian service had been. The presence of a Chabad staff member from Russia indicated that there had been interest in keeping this congregation alive. There was a group of young men at the service, all of whom were wearing American baseball caps. As a rug collector I couldn't keep my eyes off the rugs; they were beautiful.

The next morning we decided to walk around the Jewish area hoping to discover the missing women in the community and to walk through the Jewish cemetery at the edge of the community. The gravestones in the cemetery didn't seem to accept the Jewish custom of "no graven images" since there were computer pictures of the deceased on the stones. But our walk through the residential part of the community gave me a déjà vu experience. I saw women who could have been my grandmothers, dressed in garb that was quite common in the beginning of the 20th century when my family came to the U.S. One woman in particular looked just like one of my grandmothers. These women were very friendly and quite comfortable coming up to two American women with whom they couldn't really communicate because of language differences. As always, nonverbal communication techniques can work effectively.

When we returned to Baku, we decided to visit a newly constructed synagogue in the midst of the city. After the demise of the Soviet Union and the independence of Azerbaijan, the Jewish residents of the city wanted to replace old and fairly decrepit synagogue structures with a new building. There was a sizeable Jewish community in the city, many of whom had come to Baku from Russia at the turn of the 20th century when oil was discovered in the Caspian Sea. I was told that approximately ten percent of the oil companies in the early part of the century were owned by Russian Jews who had come south to make their fortunes in oil. But during the Soviet Era, the Jewish population in Baku did not fare so well. Although it seems that Jews in Azerbaijan did not experience the dramatic problems faced by other Jewish communities in the Soviet Union, they were not a thriving community at the time of independence.

It turned out that someone I met during the workshop I was conducting in Baku (who was not Jewish) had contact with several of the leaders of the Baku Jewish community. He was aware of their attempts to raise money to build a new synagogue. Evidently they explored every possible financial source they could imagine, particularly the various Jewish funds across the globe. While they were gradually accumulating resources, they were still far from the amount that they needed to begin construction. Surprisingly, they were assisted in their efforts by a contribution from the Caucasian Muslim community. I was told that this contribution allowed them to proceed.

When my friends and I visited the synagogue, we had an opportunity to meet with the man who organized the fund raising and subsequent construction process. He proudly showed us the photos of the dedication in 2003 and the officials who attended. In addition to the political figures who attended the celebration, there was a photo of three bearded men sitting in the front row. They were the Russian Orthodox bishop, the top Muslim official in the Caucuses area, and the chief rabbi of Russia. I had been told about the pre-Soviet tradition of inter-religious respect in Baku and it was clear that the Baku Jewish community drew on that convention. I was very amused, however, when I learned that the synagogue contained a small room that served as a separate prayer hall for the Georgian Jews who lived in Baku. It seemed strange that it was harder to find ways for Georgian and Azeri Jews to pray together than to raise funds from Muslim and Russian Orthodox sources.

CONTINUING TO WANDER

Over the years my experiences gave me a glimpse of what some have called a "cosmopolitan" view; that is, a sense of being a citizen of the world. But as much as I have learned from those experiences, I have really not been immersed in another society. I did spend time living a day-to-day existence in some countries but I was always an outsider. My experiences probably gave me a somewhat more substantive view of those communities than others may have had but I never really "lived" in them. But the collective result of those experiences gave me an appreciation for what we have now called a "globalized" view. It involves some ability to define differences between places and yet, at the same time, see the patterns of commonality that may actually emerge from their diverse histories and patterns of development.

My wandering has not been limited to places outside of the borders of the U.S. I have had jobs in many places in the U.S.: Aberdeen, South Dakota; Yellow Springs, Ohio; Minneapolis, Minnesota; Philadelphia, Pennsylvania; Berkeley, California; Austin, Texas; Albany, New York; and Baltimore, Maryland. But over and over again, I returned to Washington, D.C. and, after a few years, left again. So it isn't easy for me to answer the question, "Where are you from?" or "Where do you live?"

Washington, D.C. itself is not a traditional place. It is both a place of permanent residence and a place of transiency, following the constant political changes that occur in the U.S. It is a city composed of citizens who do not have "normal" political rights dealing with voting and control over their own tax-based fiscal contributions. As a result, I have never had the commitment to "place" that may be found in other cities. As such, I seem to have continued the pattern that I developed as a child in Aberdeen. I am both of the place and outside of it.

CHAPTER 7
Mother, Grandmothers, Aunts, and Feminism

It has taken me nearly eighty years to acknowledge that I am my mother's daughter. With very few exceptions, I spent most of my life defining my mother (and her influence) in very negative terms. As I look back on the choices that I made in my life, I defined my pathway as a direct rejection of the life she chose to live. I saw her as someone who as a child was intimidated by her mother and probably identified with her quiet unassuming father, the teacher. Despite her obvious intelligence and writing ability, she did not see a way to extend her formal education beyond high school. While I knew that she had lived in New York City for a decade, I viewed her return back to the Midwest as a way of copping out. She married my father, moved to a very small city in South Dakota, and had children. When my father died at a young age, she stayed in Aberdeen and focused on her two children.

This description of her life is not meant to be critical; rather it is a report of my past perceptions of her life. Indeed, as I think about it, it is really a criticism of me. While at some level I did appreciate what she did for her children, I did not ever acknowledge what she had done for us. I have regrets about this. But it is clear to me that I did not want the life that I thought she had lived. I ignored some of her attributes that I now acknowledge as positive influences on my life.

In a sense this has forced me to create two separate images of my mother. There is the person who I described in very stereotypical ways: mother, wife, housewife, and dependent. That mother was passive, dependent on others, not ambitious, and fearful of change. The other mother (whom I have recently acknowledged) was somewhat adventurous, willing to change, friendly, intellectually curious, sensitive to art and aware of her surroundings. It has been difficult for me to put those two images together.

Because I was so resistant to identifying that "other mother" as I was growing up, I looked beyond my immediate nuclear family for other women who might serve as role models for me. I first looked at my two grandmothers. My maternal grandmother was outspoken and entrepreneurial and very dissatisfied with her life and her husband. My mother was clearly intimidated by her. My paternal grandmother was passive, agreeable and willing to be taken care of by her children and her husband. My father was happy to play a major provider role as the eldest son. The two grandmothers also differed in the way that they had defined their role in a new country. One had learned English and had some contact with those outside the Jewish community while the other never learned English and probably did not live much differently in Milwaukee than she had in Byelorussia.

Since neither of those grandmothers provided me with the kind of role model I desired, I looked to my aunts as possible sources for that role. My father's three sisters did provide some elements for my quest. The eldest aunt was a born organizer who checked in with her constituency daily. She was somewhat bossy but had a good heart. She had one son who was about ten years older than I was and in many ways she treated me as the daughter she didn't have. The second aunt was a homebody who was a good cook and baker but was busy with her two children. The youngest aunt was the only person in that generation of my father's family who had attended college. She also was a good and serious cook and seemed to enjoy having a girl around her since she had two sons. Her gifts to me (particularly of clothing) represented her desire for a girl. All three of these aunts had married men who were not particularly ambitious. Eventually two of them moved to Arizona from Milwaukee. The eldest moved to Madison, Wisconsin and continued to play a role as the real head of the family. My father's younger brother's wife also provided me with some elements of a role model. She was not Jewish and her household had a more cosmopolitan perspective.

My mother's sisters never were in the running for the role model position. One of my mother's two sisters was effectively a stranger to me and the other had serious mental health problems. It was my maternal uncle's wife – Aunt Miriam – who was probably the person in the extended family who played the most important role in my life. She started me on piano lessons when I was very young and was one of the few people in my life that was able to give me the kind of advice that I was willing to accept. She often took me to concerts at the University of Minnesota when I was in town. She, my uncle and their three children had a household that I enjoyed visiting. The conversations and concerns made me feel that I was in the city and connected to the world. Especially after my father's death, we spent significant time in that home.

Despite the geographical distances between my aunts and me, in many ways their presence and influence represented the pattern of the extended family that had been found in the shtetl and other Jewish communities in Eastern Europe. It is a pattern that continues today. I realized that on my first visit to Israel. I was taking a bus in Haifa to someone's house for dinner and asked the bus driver to let me know where and when I should get off. Hearing my question, the entire bus moved into an argumentative exchange about the best location for me to disembark. At that point I realized that this was familiar to me. It seemed to me as though the entire country of Israel behaved like my family, particularly like the behavior that occurred in my grandmothers' houses. Any issue was everyone's business.

WHAT DOES IT MEAN TO BE AN AUNT?

I did value the relationship I had with my aunts. I spent time with them, learned their idiosyncrasies and styles, and was able to accept their differences. I was much less judgmental of their views and approaches than I was of my mother's. And there were specific patterns that I developed that harked back to my time with a particular aunt. For example, my Aunt Rose "checked in" with friends and family almost daily. I find myself doing the same thing but on a weekly or monthly basis.

It was interesting to me to see how each of the aunts had her own approach to cooking and baking. I started a collection of recipes from them that I have continued to use today. Each of the women had developed her own personal twist on common and familiar dishes. The recipe for apple cake that each aunt made turned out differently in each household. I learned that I could accept their differences without always agreeing with them and was able to appreciate their different life styles expressed in the kitchen and how they led their lives. As I think about it, the kitchen was also a place where I could work with my mother in a relatively comfortable fashion. Although my cooking and baking style was clearly influenced by my mother, the tension in the kitchen usually stemmed from my resistance to cleaning up after myself. But I still return to my mother's cookbooks and notes she wrote in their margins about tips in the kitchen.

The contrast between my mother and my father's sisters was clear in the way they took me shopping. Often the visits to the aunts involved shopping expeditions where an aunt was willing to be indulgent in purchases. That contrasted with shopping ventures with my mother, which were likely to result in disagreements. Visits to Aberdeen during college vacations were particularly difficult. I usually came home with my most decrepit clothing believing that would provoke my mother to take me shopping. Or, in other cases, I specifically wore something that I knew my mother didn't like. Usually my mother broke down and took me shopping. But, at least one time, she said she would take me shopping only if I would walk a few feet behind her because she didn't like what I was wearing. At the time, I did not appreciate the humor of the situation.

When my brother and his wife had two daughters I had an opportunity to think about my own role as an aunt. Even before they arrived on the scene I had developed aunt-like relationships with children of my close friends. That involved trips to the zoo, lunches at restaurants and conversations. It didn't take long for some of those children to realize, as they put it, that "we are taking Beryl to the zoo." They realized that they were an excuse for me – the adult – to go to the zoo.

I did realize that my relationship to them was similar to my relationships with my own aunts; it provided them with connections with other adults beyond their parents and immediate family. One of my favorite examples of this occurred when one of my friend's children – an eight-year-old girl – was putting names of her friends in her new telephone book. She showed me my entry – she had listed me as one of her friends. I don't think that anyone else over forty was included!

The play and film *Auntie Mame* gave me another perspective on being an aunt. I thought that the eccentricity of the main character and her atypical relationship with her nephew was an appealing model for me. As played by Rosalind Russell, Mame did not really settle down and, instead, was prone to embarking on travel adventures around the world. I don't know if my nieces thought of me as eccentric but I did try to provide them with unpredictable excursions, unusual gifts, and travel and shopping excursions when they visited me. Since one of my nieces (Anneke) had twin daughters, I have tried to continue that pattern with them.

WHAT ABOUT FEMINISM?

For women of my generation it is not easy to identify the experiences that defined our view of feminism. We were caught between changing views of the appropriate role of women in society as well as conflicts between expectations that emerged from multiple sources. My conflicting images of my mother probably exacerbated this already murky situation. As I now see it, my mother had exhibited behaviors that had more in common with the feminism of the 1930s than I had appreciated. Her decade in New York City, living in a women's residence on her own, her ability to hold a responsible administrative job in the Oriental rug business, her decision to use a different name (substituting her middle name for her first name), and her interest in art and books, did not fit the stereotype of a Midwestern Jewish woman of that era.

There were clues in her behavior that I failed to appreciate. We had books in our house library about the role of women, particularly Jewish women, and volumes about Oriental rugs. My mother stood up to the men in the Aberdeen synagogue to allow me to say Kaddish for my father along with my younger brother. When I was about twelve years old, my father's younger brother said that he would buy a bicycle for my brother. My mother told him that he couldn't buy a bicycle for my brother if he didn't also buy one for me. They eventually worked out an arrangement where my uncle paid half of the price of two bicycles to establish some sense of equity. There was a clear expectation that gender should not be used to differentiate the ways that my brother and I were treated. In fact, as the eldest child in the immediate family, there were strong expectations about what I would accomplish in school and in life.

Other ways to define feminism emerged from the other women in the family. My maternal grandmother was an angry woman who had grown up with very different expectations about her life. She knew she was smart and because she came from a prestigious rabbinical family envisioned a different life than the one that had materialized for her. I have always been intrigued by her decision to produce wine during Prohibition and sell it to the firemen who were in the fire station across the street from her house. If she had not had been responsible for a household of children, I think she would have found a way to enter the American work force. Instead, she became quite a bitter person.

My aunts provided other glimpses into possible feminism. My Aunt Rose was called Doc by her son because she was convinced that she had some expertise in health and other subjects. I have always thought that she could have been an executive director of a non-governmental organization or might have run a bureaucracy. My Aunt Miriam was someone who valued education and showed me how someone could be thoughtful and analytical and a musician, as well. Both of those women provided me with some sense of what a future life might be for a woman. But neither had created careers for themselves even though their interests and behavior might have challenged traditional views about women. Other women members of the family led lives that emphasized those roles: mother, wife, and housewife. At the same time, I clearly absorbed some of their interests. While the structure of my life is different, I am someone who is likely to have knitting or needlepoint projects underway and have always been interested in cooking and food.

As I think about feminism, I find that there are many ways to approach the topic. For me it involves at least three different issues. The first is behavioral. What is expected about your style of interacting with others in the world? Are women meant to be passive or assertive? If so, is this behavior defined by gender defined style or is it idiosyncratic to the individual? The second has to do with ambition. Does ambition reside in the individual woman? If so, is it focused on your individual goals or does it focus on goals for others (e.g. family or institutions)? The third focuses on the availability or unavailability of opportunities for a woman. Are these defined by birth, by cultural background, economic status, or by law?

These three issues are clearly intertwined. As I reflect on my life, I think that I was always balancing conflicting attributes within each of these three issues. By temperament I was assertive and outgoing. Whenever I have taken the Myers-Briggs test, based on Carl Jung's theories of personality, I come out as an ENTJ – someone who has been termed a "field marshal," who emphasizes elements from the external environment, operates intuitively, and tries to stimulate change. My energy has often been focused on goals that are not personal but more collective in their reach. And my somewhat idiosyncratic methods and concerns have sometimes faced the limitations often used devised to define a "feminist" although my values are clearly coherent with many of those attributes. Political agendas and personal issues are so intertwined that it is difficult for me to sort out the attributes of the two types of issues.

DEFINING MY OWN STYLE OF FEMINISM.

As I was growing up, I probably was more often described as the oldest child in the family rather than anything that was uniquely related to gender. But it is interesting that many of the terms used to define the "eldest child" are most often used to those defining men and not women. Achievement, responsibility, and leadership are terms that appear on both lists of attributes but have different meanings when applied to different genders. When they are found in women they are characterized in pejorative terms: bossy, controlling, and dominating. That ambiguity has always disturbed me. It is also contributed to my difficulty working out a career path.

At times I did ask the adults in my life for advice about the future. When as a high school student I spoke to the rabbi about my interest in a journalism career, he warned me about the difficulties for a woman in that field. While I was somewhat disturbed by his advice, I probably interpreted it as his inability to understand the American culture. Similarly when I asked my Antioch academic advisor about graduate school possibilities, he told me that it was better for me to go into an MA program than a PhD program because women in academia faced limitations. I accepted that advice but some ten years later did enter a PhD program. Those kinds of exchanges made me skeptical about searching for a mentor. Perhaps if I had the opportunity to work with women faculty when I was a young woman, it would have been different. But given the absence of women in higher education at that time, that was not possible. Instead I relied on friends and colleagues as sounding boards when I was considering decisions along the way.

It is hard for me to figure out when I started to identify myself as a feminist. Like my mother, I sought ways to intertwine my interest in gender issues with other interests. I was likely to look for women fiction and nonfiction writers. I was interested in the role of women in the early days of the American labor movement. I looked for some way to acknowledge the role of women in Jewish tradition. Most of the time I was looking at gender along with other concerns. My personal political agenda (some form of social change) was always combining elements – gender and race, gender and class, gender and religion.

One of my major reasons for returning to graduate school to complete a PhD when I was in my thirties was my discomfort with my job prospects. I saw a pattern in my roles; I seemed to be destined to play the role of the second person on projects. I thought that completing a doctorate would provide me with the status that would lead to leadership positions. I had no idea that I was embarking on an academic career but rather saw myself as staying in the non-academic world that I was already a part of.

THE LBJ SCHOOL

Early in my career I tended to move from job to job, from experience to experience. I did not confront the institutional biases found within professions and careers. It was not until I began an academic career at the LBJ School of Public Affairs in Austin, Texas that these issues surfaced. My years in Texas – 1973 to 1977 – coincided with the surge of interest in women's issues in the U.S. And Texas was a very interesting place to be experiencing that set of developments. Austin was in the middle of the development of the unique brand of Texas political feminism that produced Sarah Weddington and Ann Richards, two very public feminists who were important figures in the women's movement.

I came to the LBJ School in 1973 as the first and only woman faculty member. The school was only a year or two old when I arrived and the faculty I joined was a mixture of native Texas academics, Texas political figures, and individuals with particular policy expertise. I'm not sure exactly why I was selected for the job; I had just finished my PhD and evidently was seen as someone whose interest in public policy had both academic and practitioner dimensions.

The school had a new building on campus and was located next to the LBJ Presidential Library. It was relatively close to the state capitol and within sight of the university's football stadium. My job interview at the school coincided with a gala event at the LBJ Library. I discovered a few friends from Antioch in Austin and saw a woman at the event wearing the same Mexican dress that I had on. We shared compliments on our clothing taste and I thought the shared dress was a sign that I should seriously consider the position. My interview went well and I took the job.

Between my acceptance of the job and my arrival in the late summer, many changes occurred in the school. The Dean had been removed from his formal leadership position (although not from his professorial role). The turbulence that I learned was characteristic of Texas politics affected both university and state political systems. And perhaps most important, LBJ had died in the interim. He was the School's protector and with his death was no longer available to advocate for its budget or protect the school from various forms of criticisms.

I spent four years in Austin, Texas as an academic. I was the first woman faculty member hired by the LBJ School at a time when gender issues were not seen as important. I discovered that the school organized dinners for prospective faculty at a club that did not serve women when I realized that I was only invited to that club at lunchtime. When I asked the then Dean of the school if he would have agreed to organize meals at facilities that did not serve African Americans, he replied simply, "That's different."

Before I left Washington to move to Austin, a friend organized a lunch for me with several Texas natives. During the lunch, I was given some advice about living in Austin. She told me that I shouldn't underestimate the symbolism of the Texas flag: the Lone Star. It meant that Texas wasn't convinced that it was really a part of the U.S. My years in Austin convinced me of that.

While Austin was hardly "typical" of Texas, it certainly was a unique environment with a culture that was not comfortable for me. The University of Texas at Austin was in the midst of a growth period and there was an influx of individuals from outside the state hired by the academic departments. A number of those individuals were women who found ways to meet together and share perceptions of this somewhat unknown world. In that spirit, a group of about ten women met monthly to talk about their experiences. A few of the women were Texans but most of the rest of us were "Yankees," drawn from the north and west. That "Yankee" group became an important support system to individuals who found themselves trying to succeed within the highly structured academic career framework. Relatively early in the meetings of the group we discovered that each of us was the oldest child in the family and each of us had a younger brother. That generated some important shared perceptions. Some members of the group stayed in Austin and achieved tenure. Others of them – like me – left.

LBJ COLLEAGUES

As I think about my LBJ School years, they were both the best of times and the worst of times. I had some male colleagues who shared my values and approach to education. They were perfectly comfortable working with me and we developed several extremely effective policy research projects that gave students an opportunity to see the policy world through the lens of decision makers and to provide advice to those individuals. Other faculty members found it uncomfortable to have a female colleague. One elderly faculty member had difficulty figuring out what behavior was appropriate when I was around. He seemed conflicted about whether he should hold the door open for me. But my favorite example occurred when he and I got on the elevator at the same time. It was probably his custom to take off his hat when in the presence of a woman. He looked at me after taking off his hat and then quickly put it back on. I told him that he should do whatever was comfortable for him!

Some of the younger male faculty members weren't very relaxed with me or with the other woman who joined me on the faculty. The school had a very useful process of individually reviewing the progress of the first-year students at the end of the first year. The process usually involved meetings that lasted two or three days. Faculty who had taught the students during the year would share their assessment of the student. One young faculty member was describing his students and came to one young woman. He described her as follows: "She is an attractive blond who I didn't think had a brain in her head. But she surprised me that she did very good work." I sat there and waited until it was my turn. I was focusing on a young male student. I said: "He was so good looking and muscular that I didn't think he had a brain in his body." Some of my colleagues started to laugh but the young faculty member didn't seem to get it.

While I was an official part of the faculty, I often felt as if I was an outsider in the system. The faculty meetings were long and often made me feel somewhat alien in the group. At one point I decided that I would bring my knitting to the meetings. I was working on a baby outfit for a friend and started it at the beginning of the meeting. By the end of the several day sessions, I had completed the outfit. That seemed to me to be a good use of my time. However, several of my colleagues commented on the process, expressing their discomfort with my knitting. I realized that I had communicated a desire to be outside the group when one person said, "You completed a knitted garment; what did we accomplish?" There were other instances in my life when bringing my knitting or needlepoint work to a professional setting was probably not a good idea. When artist Judy Chicago developed the Dinner Party project (a ceremonial banquet, arranged on a triangular table with a total of thirty-nine place settings, each commemorating an important woman from history) I welcomed her willingness to use traditional women's needlework techniques as an essential part of the artwork.

I seem to have expressed my differences with the local norms in other more substantive ways. At that point in time the University was effectively a white institution. There were very few students of color or students from Hispanic backgrounds in the student body. I became one of the advocates for the creation of a committee on women and minorities attached to the Faculty Senate and was eventually appointed to chair that committee. We conducted the first analysis of hiring and promotion patterns across the campus and disseminated the analysis fairly widely. Because this was my first encounter with the politics of the academic world, I did not stop to calculate the possible effects that this activity would have on my possibilities of achieving tenure.

Because I was somewhat older than a traditional untenured assistant professor, I was impatient about waiting for the seven-year calendar of service to play out before going up for tenure. At that point my dissertation had already been converted to a book and was accepted for publication; that, plus some other publications, seemed to meet the publications expectation from the university. The publication record plus my teaching evaluations and university and professional service gave me the mistaken judgment that I could go up for tenure in my fifth year, rather than the seventh year. The rejection of my tenure request made me realize that it is too easy for academic institutions to use the formal requirements as a way of denying tenure for women. That experience was painful and certainly changed the approach that I used later when I was seeking tenure (which I received) from three other institutions.

My four years in Austin represented an education in the patterns of institutionalized gender discrimination. In addition to the behavioral expectations associated with the academic world, I started to notice other patterns. When I looked at the citations that were used in publications, I began to see that male academics rarely cited women (although women almost always cited men). Panels and presentations at conferences of the time were frequently all male. Women participation often began in panels dealing specifically with women's issues. At one political science conference I ran into an acquaintance I knew from Washington who asked me what I was doing at the conference. I told him that I was on a panel dealing with women's political issues. He replied, "This isn't a gynecological conference."

Attention to patterns of gender discrimination grew during this period and a literature emerged that was both intellectually important but also useful to women in formerly all-male settings. When I read Deborah Tannen's book, *You Just Don't Understand*, I was struck by her discussion of patterns of interruption. She noted that women tend to be interrupted more than men and that women who interrupt are seen more negatively than men who do it. I began to understand that women often view conversations as collective experiences where the participants talk along with each other. In contrast, men are more likely to see their contributions as individual presentations. Others described the failure of a mixed gender group to acknowledge the contributions of the women present and, instead, to ascribe ideas to some male participant. In fact, there is a belief that women have to say something three times before their position is acknowledged.

MY PERSONAL STYLE OF FEMINISM

Although my own substantive research agenda does not usually focus on classic feminist issues, I have tried to devise approaches that provide a way for me to pass on my concern about the role of women. I have tried to avoid the kind of stereotyping that I was guilty of in my early perception of my mother. As I have approached my role as a teacher, I have spent a lot of time and energy as a mentor to a younger generation of women (and often men as well). I have been someone who is quick to comment about panels and publications that only involve men; I don't let that observation go unspoken. I have tried to balance my approaches in ways that are strategic but, at the same time, provide a way for me to be clear about my values. That doesn't always work; sometimes I can't keep my thoughts to myself or the others involved are just too resistant to change to even hear me. And most of all, I have tried to identify gender issues and link them to other value concerns. That has allowed me to balance gender with issues of race, income and other social issues. That is not easy to do and becomes difficult when trying to achieve coalitions of support. But it is a good example of my attempt to live in multiple worlds.

CHAPTER 8
Israel

I was twelve years old when Israel was created. But it seems to me that I always knew that would happen. Like many other families, my family was conscious about the strong relationship between Zionism (the movement for the establishment and development of a Jewish nation) and the realities of the Holocaust and World War II. I knew that there had been members of both sides of my family who were focused on Palestine and a homeland for Jews; I later learned that distant relatives had gone to Palestine from Belarus (formerly Byelorussia) around the same time that my grandparents came to the U.S. And I assumed that others did not survive the Holocaust.

Also like many other families, we were expected to collect money for the Jewish National Fund and place it in the small blue box visible on the kitchen shelves. During World War II, birthdays and other commemorations were not only marked by the purchase of U.S. savings bonds but also by the purchase of trees for the forestation in Israel sponsored by the Jewish National Fund. I've recently learned that tree planting is an ancient Jewish tradition. Evidently a Talmudic rabbi used to say that if a person planting a tree heard that the Messiah had arrived, he should finish planting before going to greet him. In my mind, I saw a natural affinity between efforts to plant a victory garden in the U.S. during World War II and efforts to support planting trees in Israel around the same time.

My mother was a strong supporter of Hadassah, the Zionist women's organization founded by Henrietta Szold. I thought of Szold's work as the global activist expression of the values of poet Emma Lazarus whose poetry is found on the Statue of Liberty. After the creation of the state of Israel my mother focused on the need to sell Bonds for Israel. There were yearly Bonds for Israel dinners in Aberdeen and the small Aberdeen congregation turned out to have one of the highest per capita contributions of funds in the country during the 1950s. One of my uncles bought enough bonds to receive the sixteen-volume edition of *The Encyclopedia Judaica* as a complimentary gift. (That Encyclopedia is an English language encyclopedia that covers Jewish history of all eras, culture, holidays, language, scripture and religious teachings.) When he was no longer able to take care of himself and went into a nursing home, I received that shelf long set.

To me, there was a link between the promises attached to immigration to the U.S. and the promises attached to Zionism. Rather than setting up a conflict between the two, I tended to see them as representing similar values and hopes. It was not surprising that I became an enthusiastic supporter of J Street years later. (J Street is a nonprofit group in the U.S. that seeks to promote American leadership to end the Arab-Israel and Israel-Palestinian conflicts.). But there were many years and a number of tests along the way that challenged the views I had about Israel.

ZIONIST CAMP

Israel moved from an abstraction to reality during the years I attended Herzl Camp, a Zionist camp about 100 miles from Minneapolis. The camp recruited young people mostly from Minneapolis and St. Paul but it also brought campers from parts of Illinois and both North and South Dakota to this wooded area in Wisconsin. The founding director of the camp was a rabbi from Minneapolis who combined Jewish religious traditions with the Zionist ideology that soon resulted in the creation of Israel. The camp opened just two years before Israel became a reality and drew many of its staff from what was then Palestine.

I was intrigued by the combination of the religious and political agendas that emerged from the three or four week long summer experience. One description of the camp noted that, "From the beginning, athletics, waterfront activities, recreation, music, dancing, cultural and creative events were all components of the Herzl experience." While I wasn't particularly interested in the athletics part of the program, I did thrive on the color war structure of the camp efforts. I think that was the first time I thought of myself as someone who could play a leadership role with my peers. I found it very exciting to learn that the activities we were highlighting at camp were the very activities that would be found in Israel. We saw the structure of the camp as similar to a kibbutz and the campers were given responsibilities for taking care of a garden, cleaning facilities and were involved in keeping the dining room and kitchen going. The Israeli interpretation of traditional religious activities was refreshing and gave me a new perspective on the Sabbath services. It was one thing to have a ceremony at the end of the Sabbath in your home or synagogue. But when that ceremony occurred outside and involved dramatic ways of lighting a campfire, it seemed to be magical. Most of the Hebrew words that I continue to recognize today emerged from the activities at camp and the music and dance built into the day-to-day routines.

It wasn't ever clear to me whether the counselors from Palestine (and then Israel) were actually committed to the religious element in the camp program. My memory is that they were largely secular and they were focused on building a nation. We had a glimpse of the effort to find Hebrew names for modern places and activities. My favorite example was the Hebrew name for the toilet. It was *bet ha keesay* – house of the chair.

I really loved that camp and continued to attend it during my high school years. It seemed obvious to me that I would become a junior counselor when I started college. The summer after my first year at Antioch was somewhat disjointed since I tried to reconcile the values and approaches I had been exposed to at college with some of the traditional religious observations at Herzl. I did find an unusual similarity between life in Yellow Springs and camp when I discovered that both areas served 3.2 beer to individuals under twenty-one. My days off at camp usually involved a trip with other counselors to local bars where we were able to order Leinenkugel beer, one of the few brands that provided what was called "low-point" beer. The Olde Trail Tavern in Yellow Springs also served a low point brand. That seemed to be the only similarity between the two places. Mostly I was struck by the differences between my life at camp and that at Antioch. Antioch had placed me in a more cosmopolitan world while Herzl returned me to variations on familiar traditions.

Despite my skepticism about traditional Judaism, I continued to be interested in finding a way to link that interest with my academic work. While working on my master's degree at the University of Minnesota, I took a course from sociologist Arnold Rose on Jewish communities in the U.S.

Throughout my teens and twenties, whenever I was somewhat depressed and unsure about the direction my life was taking, I thought about going to Israel. I didn't have any illusions about going home if "home" meant South Dakota. Although I had no real information about Israel, I had created a view about it that moved the image of Israel as a homeland for all Jews to a personal home for me. Luckily, I did not have serious bouts of depression and the idea of going to Israel remained an abstract and symbolic possibility. But my first and subsequent visits to Israel tested those ideas.

ISRAEL IN 1966

I used my year living in London as a convenient way to explore Europe and Israel. In addition to my train trip to the USSR I took a train journey across Europe through the former Yugoslavia to arrive in Greece. After exploring much of the Greek mainland and the major Greek islands I moved to my final destination: Israel. I took a boat from the Greek port of Piraeus to Haifa. As we moved through the Mediterranean, past Cyprus, I felt that I was replaying the experience of the World War II survivors who had arrived in Palestine on the boat, SS Exodus. The pictures I had seen of that journey showed an overflow of people on the boat, many of whom stayed on the deck of the ship throughout the journey to capture their first glimpse of the "Promised Land". The young people who were on my boat did the same thing and I found the experience incredibly moving. When the boat docked in Haifa I couldn't believe that all of the people who were working at the docks were Jews. I had never thought of Jews as stevedores and employed as dockworkers. They certainly weren't found in Brando's *On The Waterfront*.

But when I found the small hotel that I had booked in Haifa, I discovered a familiar environment. One of the guests in the hotel was the individual who had been the secretary of the Israeli cabinet. After his retirement he had organized efforts to tutor new immigrants to Israel and provide them with extra help in learning the Hebrew language. He was in Haifa to accompany a group of young Israelis to an Ulpan (a place for intensive study of Hebrew) where they would spend the day as tutors for individuals who found the language difficult. Conversations at small hotels were easy to develop, especially when the hotel guests shared a breakfast table. On my first day in Israel, this man was interested in my involvement in the U.S. civil rights movement and I was intrigued by his project. He invited me to join the young Israelis and travel to the Ulpan riding on the back of a pickup truck.

I started a conversation with a woman (about my age) who was sitting next to me in the truck. I realized she was an American and learned that she was from Chicago and was teaching in Jerusalem. She asked me where I was from. I said South Dakota, knowing that this response usually stopped any further questioning. But she didn't stop there. She asked me, "Where in South Dakota?" That was an unusual response. When I said "Aberdeen," she asked me whether I knew her family, the Ribnicks. Of course I knew them. It was indeed a small world. She invited me to stay with her in Jerusalem and in later years when we were both living in Washington and involved in activities supporting the Israeli peace movement, we remembered that exchange.

That first day in Israel began a very interesting visit about three weeks long. I had friends from Philadelphia who had returned to Israel and were academics in Jerusalem. They had both been young people in the Hagganah, the paramilitary organization during the war of Independence that became the basis for the Israeli Defense Force. I spent time with them in Jerusalem but also went with them on the back road between Jerusalem and Tel Aviv that suffered extensive losses of both lives and military hardware during the War of Independence. At the time of my visit, the road was still littered with trucks, tanks, and other vehicles. We also visited a kibbutz (a collective community in Israel that was traditionally based on agriculture) in the north that was affiliated with a left wing political party. I learned that the further left the kibbutz was in terms of its politics, the more it invested in the design and development of the collective areas of the kibbutz rather than in individual dwellings. One of my friend's relatives lived on a moshav, a cooperative rather than collective body. Visiting those relatives gave me a sense of the differences between the two forms of settlements; the former focused on collective activity while the other allowed residents to maintain separate households.

A friend of a friend lived in a kibbutz just below the border with Lebanon and I visited him there. At that time, this was a kibbutz that had good relationships with the Bedouin tribes in the area and we were invited to have coffee with some members of the Bedouin community that was brewed over the campfire. I traveled from the northern tip of the country to the most southern area, going through the desert to Eilat on the Gulf of Aqaba. I took tours of the country and was especially aware of the limitations of my movements within Jerusalem. I looked into East Jerusalem from the window of a church at the border and was stunned when I realized that I was looking directly at a gun that was pointed at me. And when I was walking around the Mea Sharim neighborhood in Jerusalem (the area where the most Orthodox Jews lived at the time) I was chastised because I was going into the area wearing a sleeveless top. That led to my quip that I was against the right to bear (bare) arms – except when in Israel.

When in Tel Aviv I stayed in a small hotel owned and operated by people who had come to Palestine from Germany between the two World Wars. Although they had been in Israel for more than thirty years, they still didn't speak Hebrew fluently. They were more comfortable speaking to me in English than in Hebrew. That gave me a different picture of assimilation than I had assumed.

That first trip to Israel didn't clarify my views about the country.

But it was the only place I'd been where I avoided being told that I didn't look Jewish. I was uncomfortable being in a place where anxiety was built into day-to-day behaviors. Even the way that Israelis smoked their cigarettes expressed that anxiety. But I found it fascinating to be in an environment that was familiar to me in some ways (for example, social and family behaviors) but didn't understand in other ways.

MY SECOND VISIT IN THE MID 1970S

Less than a decade later I made my second visit to Israel. Much had changed during that period since the borders of Israel had shifted as a result of the Six Day War in 1967. I had learned of an organization called American Professors for Peace in the Middle East that organized trips for academicians over the Christmas holidays. Approximately a dozen academics had registered for the trip. As it turned out we travelled with a similar Australian group. I knew a few of the American individuals, all of whom were Jewish. I wasn't sure of that when the trip began. At least one of the participants didn't seem to have much of an identity with Judaism at the beginning. As the trip progressed, after a few days he started wearing a small Star of David around his neck. By the end of the trip, he was wearing a heavy chain with a Star that measured about a foot in length. I guess that trip had an impact on his identity.

The Australians on the trip were much more interesting. All were Jewish but represented very different migration patterns to Australia. That group sparked my interest in visiting Australia (something I did a few years later). Several were descendants of the original convicts brought to Australia; I was convinced that they probably were guilty of white-collar crimes. Others had come during World War II as refugees and were a part of the original development of the political science field in Australia. And still others were relatively recent migrants and came during the Cold War. One individual was Polish and did not know he was Jewish during the Communist era. As a child living in a Soviet society, his parents did not tell him anything about his Jewish ancestry but he eventually learned about it. He came to Australia after completing his academic work in Poland and became more interested in his background. I walked around Yad Vashem (the Holocaust Museum) with him and experienced his introduction to the substance of these exhibits. He focused on the photos of Polish communities before the War while I kept returning to a map that showed Jewish communities before the Holocaust. I found the towns that my parents came from. Seeing them on the map allowed me to have a sense of reality about their early life that I had never experienced before.

This was the first time that I was able to move around much of Jerusalem. I was able to go to the ancient Temple Mount that was in the eastern part of the city. I saw the original campus of Hebrew University that was not accessible in the past. We were able to shop in Palestinian open-air bazaars. Unlike my first trip, this was an organized program that provided us with an opportunity to meet with various political figures. We met with Moshe Dayan (an important Israel military leader and politician) and a number of parliamentarians and were able to visit some of the territory that had been claimed by Israel during the Six Day War. We were taken to the Golan Heights and walked through a deserted bunker that was still decorated with pictures of pinup women that were similar to the photos that the GIs in World War II had posted on their bunker walls. During one excursion, the group of U.S. and Australian academics sat on a site on a mountaintop and talked to our guide about these changes. I can still hear him tell us, "There is no such thing as a good occupation." That comment continues to be prophetic.

THE FIRST INTIFADA; MY THIRD TRIP. 1988

The First Intifada – the Palestinian uprising against the Israeli occupation of the Palestinian territories – began at the end of 1987 and lasted for four or five years. That development spawned a new American response to the political and military actions taken by the Israeli government. It made me and many others concerned about the behaviors by the Israel government that seemed to have contributed to the uprising. We became more aware of the activities of an Israeli organization called Peace Now (Shalom Achshav). This group was formed in a response to a letter to the Prime Minister of Israel from nearly 350 reserve officers and soldiers from the Israeli army calling for a two-nation solution that included both Israel and Palestine. To me and others with similar views, it was time for Americans to support those in Israel who did not agree with the policies of the current Israeli government. Within days of the Intifada development, a group was formed in Washington as a part of the American Peace Now movement, calling for the evacuation of settlements in the Palestinian territory and the creation of a separate Palestinian state to operate in an environment of peace. A daylong conference was held at American University, bringing together a rather diverse group of people who agreed with the Peace Now agenda. That event became the first major activity of a group that continues to thrive today.

When Peace Now offered its membership an opportunity to visit Israel, I jumped at the possibility. This trip gave me a chance to meet a new generation of Israeli leaders and to visit a country that was very different than the one I had visited in the past. We met in a facility that looked directly at the wall that had divided the two sections of Jerusalem. We met with Palestinian leaders in the beautiful American Colony hotel in East Jerusalem. One of my former students was spending the year in Israel and she arrived at my hotel wearing combat boots and carrying a rifle. It was hard for me to see her emergence from peace activist in the U.S. to someone who had embraced the military side of the Israeli experience. She was living in a border community at the northern tip of Israel where attacks were common.

My experience walking around Jerusalem was very different than it had been in the past. Because of the changes in the Soviet system, Russian migrants were very visible. It was painful to see a woman playing her violin on the streets to earn money, accompanied by her husband. It turned out that she had been the concertmistress of a symphony orchestra in Russia and couldn't find a similar position in Israel. At one meeting with some Russian immigrants, I asked a middle-aged man trained as an engineer about his life. I won't forget his remark: "In Russia I was a successful engineer. In Israel I am nothing." While immigration anywhere in the world is almost always a difficult transition, I didn't expect that in Israel. And Jerusalem had shifted from one of the most beautiful cities

I had seen to a place where the beauty was overshadowed by an aggressive religious community that made me feel that I didn't belong there.

We saw the less humane results of the occupation. We were taken to one of the new settlements in the Palestinian territory. That settlement was formed by a group of New York City orthodox families who believed that they had an historical right to live on the land that was a part of the ancient boundaries of Judea and Samaria. It was chilling to hear the leaders of the settlement demand their right to continue to take over land that was also the land of ancient Palestinians. I felt that the possibility of convincing those individuals that they were living in the end of the 20th century (not in the 17th century or even earlier) was very unlikely.

A few days later we visited a house in the outskirts of Jerusalem that was owned by a Palestinian family. It was a three-floor dwelling that in the past had provided housing for three families. Somehow, when one of the families moved out of the top dwelling, a group of young Israelis managed to move in. Their goal was to drive out the other two – Palestinian – families by playing loud music all day and all night. The music was rigged up into loudspeakers that not only interrupted the lives of the two families in the house but also all of their neighbors. The constant noise was really inhumane and didn't seem to me to be what I thought was appropriate Jewish behavior.

When I went with friends to a Lebanese restaurant in Tel Aviv, I had trouble comprehending the menu. I asked the owner what language the menu was using; he said it was in Hebrew and English. But as a regular patron of Lebanese cuisine, I didn't recognize the English terms. It turned out that the English used was the Anglicized version of Hebrew that resulted from transliteration. When I realized that, I asked him if I could use the Arabic names of foods since that's what I was used to. So I asked him about babaganuch, humos and other familiar dishes. He thought it was quite funny that an American Jew wanted to order in Arabic, not in Hebrew or in Hebrew converted into English.

I left Israel feeling that my romanticized views about Israel were shattered. I saw a country that I felt was a part of my life turn into something that I didn't recognize. I could not operate as someone with double standards. I felt that the values that motivated both my professional and civic lives in the U.S. were being challenged by what I saw in Israel. It reminded me of the disjuncture I had seen growing up in a Jewish community in South Dakota between the values of some members of the community and that of my family. I didn't expect to return to Israel again.

RETURNING TO ISRAEL IN 2013

More than twenty years elapsed between the Peace Now trip and the world of the 21st century. During that time I explored other parts of the world, discovering interesting professional practices and almost always finding a way to uncover unusual Jewish communities in those areas. While I moved around the globe, I tended to return again and again to a few locations: Australia and India and more recently Hong Kong. My limited language abilities made those three English-speaking areas relatively easy to manage. I was able to bring my professional identity to these visits and to find ways to interact with other elements of those societies. My fields of policy analysis and public management were becoming increasingly globalized and I began attending conferences and meetings outside of the U.S. I didn't see how that focus would lead me back to Israel. I was more interested in learning about the communities that were a part of the two Diasporas from the destruction of the First and Second Temples in Jerusalem. I became intrigued with literatures and films that sought to trace the 10 lost tribes of Israel, especially those tribes that moved into regions that were not linked to European Jewry. As someone who grew up in a nontraditional Jewish environment, I felt a level of identification with what I called "Jews from strange places."

In the meantime, I didn't drop my concern about the future of Israel. In 2008 the creation of J Street provided me with an organizational setting that expressed my most basic concern: how could I link the values that motivated me as an American citizen with my identity as a Jew? I clearly responded to the organization's description:

> "J Street is the political home for pro-Israel, pro-peace Americans fighting for the future of Israel as the democratic homeland of the Jewish people. We believe that Israel's Jewish and democratic character depend on a two-state solution, resulting in a Palestinian state living alongside Israel in peace and security. Rooted in our commitment to Jewish and democratic values, J Street is redefining what it means to be pro-Israel in America. We are changing the U.S. political dynamics around Israel by mobilizing broad support for a two-state solution because it's in Israel's and America's interest. And we are expanding support for Israel by affirming – along with many Israelis – that being pro-Israel doesn't require supporting every policy of its government."

I found it both whimsical and moving that the organization used the name of J Street even though there was not a J Street on the Washington map between I Street and K Street. J Street became visible in Washington both literally and figuratively and provided a place for individuals like me to express their views.

When I attended J Street's second annual conference, I also saw that the organization had the ability to reach a generation of young people who were in colleges and universities. Since that first conference (and the subsequent conferences that I have attended) I have been impressed with those young people who are a part of the J Street University structure and found on more than fifty campuses. They bring a perspective to the situation that I believe is both effective today and also provides a sense of involvement for the future.

Despite my commitment to the two-state strategy through J Street, I had not expected to return to Israel again. My last experience there had been difficult and I thought that it made sense for me to emphasize the American perspective on the Middle East issues. But that changed when I met a few Israeli academics at an international political science conference in Madrid. I found that Tel Aviv University had a thriving public policy program and the director of the program was interested in finding a way for me to visit them.

That invitation seemed to offer me a different way of approaching Israel than I had experienced in the past. I would not be a tourist or a Zionist coming to Israel. I would be an academic who shared professional concerns with faculty in another academic setting. And I found it more appealing to be located in Tel Aviv rather than in Jerusalem. We arranged for me to make a visit over Thanksgiving. However, that visit was rescheduled because of rocket attacks on Israel during that period. Instead I visited the program over my spring break.

I had a wonderful time during that too short visit. I lectured to three different classes and was impressed with the students there. Two of the classes were composed of full time students while the third was an executive program for adults who wanted to complete a master's degree in policy. I asked the forty plus students in the executives' class to introduce themselves and tell me where they worked. As we moved around the classroom I learned that the participants worked in the Prime Minister's Office, the Israeli Defense Force, local government bodies, and quite a few non-government organizations. One of the last people to give an introduction turned out to be the woman who directed the J Street Office in Jerusalem.

My teaching style usually involves exercises done in small groups. I used that technique in all three class settings. The younger students were more compliant in responding to my instructions. Not surprisingly, the class of executives really got into the assignment and the noise level in the classroom became quite intense. All of a sudden I burst out in Hebrew, "Shekhet bivakasha" – the term that asks people to keep quiet or somewhat politely asks them to shut up. I hadn't used that term since my days at Herzl camp more than fifty years earlier. But the atmosphere in the classroom seemed to evoke that memory and bring my little knowledge of Hebrew back. The class appreciated my verbal memory.

During the visit I spent time with the faculty, particularly the younger faculty. I stayed in a hotel off the beach and was struck by the similarities between Tel Aviv and Los Angeles. The friends from Philadelphia that I had visited during my first trip to Israel had moved to Tel Aviv from Jerusalem and we enjoyed catching up. My host at the University and her husband joined me to see the film, *The Gatekeepers*, the documentary story of Shin Bet, the Israeli internal security service. We travelled outside of the city to attend a performance of one of Israel's very creative modern dance groups. I began to realize that the wave of Russian emigration brought more than musicians to the country and that Israel's preemptive position involving technology was linked to a generation of new settlers from Russia who came with technical skills.

Tel Aviv did allow me to escape from some of my negative memories of past visits. But those old views were joined by new uncomfortable experiences. The hotel staff had a number of staff who were African refugees to Israel and were living in an uncertain situation because of policies of the Israeli government. My visit to the Diaspora Museum that is part of the Tel Aviv University campus demonstrated to me how difficult it has been for those in power in Israel to acknowledge that Jews come with different and diverse ethnic and racial backgrounds. When I walked through the Museum's permanent collection, I couldn't find one photo of a non-white person even though Israel has residents from India, Ethiopia, and other non-European areas. I haven't returned to the museum but am told that there is now a new museum that represents an effort to put diaspora Jews on an equal footing with those in Israel.

Although I had expected to stay only in Tel Aviv on this visit, I wanted to see the daughter of some close friends who was living in Jerusalem with her husband and their three children. She was the development director for the Hand-in-Hand schools – a group of schools with a student body that was half Israeli Jewish and half Israeli Arab with classes taught in both Hebrew and Arabic.

In the short time I was in Jerusalem I was shocked by the way that Jerusalem and its environs had changed; no longer was this a magical city that emerged from the hills built with the same materials that came from the hillsides. The remnants of vehicles from the 1940s that were put on the edge of highways to mark the independence movement seemed to be of little interest to people. Several huge yeshivas had been built on hillsides in materials and designs that were quite unattractive. Once we arrived at my friend's neighborhood, I saw the West Bank Barrier from their balcony. That wasn't the Jerusalem I remembered from my first visit.

BACK TO TEL AVIV: 2016

Three years elapsed between my fourth visit and a return to Israel for a research symposium on Policy Analysis in Israel at Tel Aviv University. The meeting was subtitled "Piecing Together the Policy Analysis Puzzle in a Volatile Environment" and was described as a celebration of the publication of a book on policy analysis in Israel. The workshop itself was fascinating as it included presentations by a number of people who had contributed to the volume. Along with an academic from Germany, I was asked to comment on the volume and other books on policy analysis across the globe.

I am always wary of being an American Jew who tries to give advice to Israelis. I sought to use my knowledge of the policy analysis field in a comparative perspective to suggest some patterns that may transcend political borders. I noted that I was a first generation American Jew who was brought up in South Dakota – an unusual place for someone with my family's background. I tried to provide an alternative argument to that found in the book. Most of the contributors seemed to argue that policy analysis in Israel is sui generis and is unique because of the context in which it takes place. The description of that context usually views Israel as a country almost always at war, a population constantly growing and becoming more diverse, and a place with internal religious and political battles. My remarks were premised on my belief that policy analysis in Israel has more in common with the activity in other countries than may be realized or acknowledged. I focused on changes that had occurred in other countries (including the U.S.) that raised a number of questions that frame tensions in both Israel and other countries. The participants in the workshop included people from groups representing those who supported a two-state approach and concern about the application of democratic principles to the Israel Arab population.

Evidently, my tone seemed convincing to the participants in the workshop and I escaped the Israeli style of confrontation. When I described my concern to a friend, he noted, "Being yelled at is no fun, though when Israelis do it you can discount it a lot because it's the local sport, nothing personal."

While this part of the trip turned out to be positive, my reactions concerning the mood in Israel were not. During the three years that had elapsed since my last trip things had changed. Walking around Tel Aviv I saw evidence that Tel Aviv's characterization as a secular city had been eroded. Young men from yeshivot were walking around the city. While they weren't as dominant in Tel Aviv as in Jerusalem, one had the sense that secularism wasn't as obvious as it had been in the past. Disparities between the rich and the poor were apparent in the separation of housing for residents. Gated communities may have been justified for security reasons but also showed class disparities.

Overall the mood of the city had changed. It was clear to me that violence had permeated the city. Indeed, while I was there, four Israelis were killed in a trendy shopping center in Tel Aviv. One of these individuals was a friend of a former doctoral student of mine. Tension was expressed in many ways. Staff members at the hotel and restaurants were clearly fearful of the political shifts that were taking place in the government and had difficulty focusing on the problems of their clients. I was told that the average size of young families was moving from three children to four children. It wasn't clear why that was occurring; was it evidence of religious beliefs, was it an acknowledgement of the uncertainty about life, or something else? Friends tried to ignore the uncertainties surrounding them and several focused on personal health problems rather than the signals coming from the external environment. While that wasn't strange for people of my age, it seemed to be hard for many Israelis to think about the future.

WHAT IS NEXT?

It is painful for me to think about Israel's future. During my lifetime I have experienced many disparate visions of that country. I am uncertain about which vision will prevail. I like to think of myself as a realist but it pains me to see how the current Israeli government has embarked on what seems to be a self-destructive path. I've moved far from the little girl who wanted to put her coins in the JNF blue box or buy trees to plant in Israel. But I still want to invoke that memory even though it is difficult.

PART III

Crafting a Career

CHAPTER 9
Crafting a Career: Early Stages

As long as I can remember I didn't have an answer to the question "What do you want to be when you grow up?" The question seemed to demand an answer that I thought was unknowable. I knew that I didn't want to stay in Aberdeen but I had no idea what that meant. I did know that education was the vehicle one used to find a way to think about the future. But I had no sense about the pathways one might take to achieve either personal or professional goals. While my uncertain approach to the future clearly was an expression of my personal experience of loss (particularly my father's death), my views about a career were not particularly unusual for a first generation American or a woman in the 1950s.

In at least part of my mother's family, learning for its own sake was viewed as intrinsically valuable. Many of the next generation of that family translated this set of values into legal careers. My father's family was more likely to think about possibilities in business. But neither of these pathways was viewed as a serious possibility for a woman of my generation. And I seemed unable to appreciate the way that both of my parents found a way to balance their desire to become Americans along with the values embedded in their eastern European beginnings.

As I reflect on this, while my views about the future were probably idiosyncratic, I did not grow up in an environment where students in high school clearly thought about their future careers. It was more likely that they thought about jobs, not careers. And the American belief in progress provided them with the belief that they would surpass their parents in both status and economic possibilities. I've never tried to analyze this pattern but it is my sense that most of the girls in my class assumed that they were likely to be public school teachers and wives and mothers in the future.

The jobs held by members of the Jewish community in Aberdeen didn't provide alternative examples of careers. The retail establishments (ladies ready-to-wear stores, grocery stores, and army surplus stores) owned by the older generation were sometimes passed on to their children. But it was not uncommon in other families for other children to leave town for college and never return. I always thought that I would be in that group. By the time I was in junior high school I was intrigued by the experience of a distant cousin who had been elected to the South Dakota State Senate. He owned a store on Main Street but was best known for his civic role. My household and the extended family in Minneapolis and Milwaukee were places where political discussions were frequently the subject of conversations. But that didn't really give me a clue about how I would express those interests in my future.

I have a very strong memory of taking the Kuder Preference Test in the 7th grade. This test is designed to help students think about the future; the answers in the test seek to help students decide what courses they would take in junior high school and high school. It was assumed that this would structure patterns of interest that would, in turn, allow a student to translate them into career choices. I found the questions and choices very strange. I remember saying cynically that the Kuder test asked you to decide whether you would like to make a brick, throw a brick, or build a brick wall. I had trouble figuring out what that would tell me.

My skepticism was reinforced by the test results I received. I was told that I was interested in two possible careers. One was to be a U.S. Senator. The other was to be a musician. While these two possible pathways did reflect my diverse interests, they did not do much to help me think about the future. There seemed to be a real difference between personal interests and careers. And I knew enough about the difficulties in both politics and music fields to know that interest didn't guarantee a job. While I was interested in both of those possibilities, I didn't have the motivation to organize my future life around those specific goals.

WHAT WAS I INTERESTED IN?

It was dawning on me during junior high school that my career possibilities didn't fit the traditional list of professions and fields. There were things that I liked – but they weren't among the usual list. Insights began to emerge but they were not likely to be found in job announcements.

I knew that I wanted to be in an environment where politics, current events, and books were discussed and valued. I was especially attracted to reading books written by women (e.g. Nancy Drew, Louisa May Alcott, Laura Ingalls Wilder).

I began to understand that it was difficult for me to focus narrowly on one set of issues. During high school I was involved in several music forums, the student organization, and the Girl Scouts. I was easily bored with a single topic. I sought to make a difference.

My interests were stimulated and reinforced by activity that took place in a collective or group setting. I liked accompanying other musicians on the piano and sharing these experiences with others. Similarly, I thrived on group experiences in summer camps. While my travel opportunities were somewhat limited, I saw travel as an adventure and enjoyed learning about different environments.

From high school years onward it was difficult for me to characterize my path of development. Was it simply responding to targets of opportunity or did it have some structure? I tried many different opportunities. Sometimes it seemed as if I were trying on different costumes to see which one suited my style. I found experiences that were more likely to tell me what I didn't want to do rather than to give me clues for the future. The word "networking" had not yet appeared in the vocabulary but it was clear that my tendency to move from place to place provided me with a setting that allowed me to develop close friendships and colleagues in many places.

As I noted earlier, my choice of Antioch for my undergraduate education seemed to fit my interests perfectly. The stars seemed to be in alignment when I was told about the college by my aunt and found a few others who knew about it even in South Dakota. My commitment to that unusual college in Ohio actually began the minute I walked on the campus. It was clear to me that I had made the right selection of a college and never had second thoughts about that choice. I learned that my interest agenda meshed with the structure of the Antioch system. Antioch did emphasize concerns about politics and social change; taking ideas and academic work seriously; focusing on multiple issues and fields (including music and art along with traditional academic fields); and defining education as both an individual and group experience. My time on campus coincided with the inchoate stages of the Civil Rights Movement and followed the impact of World War II veterans on the culture of the campus. I was on campus during the 1956 presidential campaign and joined colleagues in an excursion to hear Democratic candidate Adlai Stevenson speak in another part of Ohio. That experience showed me that politics involved more than voting once or twice a year.

I completed my undergraduate education very satisfied with the four years I spent at the school. My first year was spent entirely on campus but the other three years included both campus classes and job placements. And my year at the University of Minnesota working on a master's degree in American Studies extended that positive experience. But I still did not have a vocabulary that allowed me to describe what I would consider a career path.

THE PHILADELPHIA YEARS

I left the academic environment in 1959 (only to return to it about a decade later). It was fortuitous for me to land in Philadelphia just as the 60s were about to bloom. I had decided to go to Philadelphia for several reasons. First, I had very close friends from Antioch who were living there who shared many of my interests and concerns. Second, I thought that the presence of a stellar American Studies program at the University of Pennsylvania gave me the possibility of returning to school if I wanted to take that pathway. But I really had no idea of the potential opportunities available in the City of Brotherly Love.

It didn't take me long to find my first job in Philadelphia. Because of the Antioch work experience I had a resume that suggested I was likely to be useful in some setting. I was living near the University and somehow heard of a job opening at the University's Medical School working on a project on treating depression. The psychiatrist leading the research was among those who were linking individual psychological issues to issues and problems in the larger environment. I was able to listen to sessions with patients whose depression symptoms were clearly related to their life realities. I realized that the racial and economic problems they experienced would cause anyone to be depressed. I saw that it was hard to separate the personal from broader social issues. The experience with that job was interesting but seemed to be tangential to my real interests.

As a result, my tenure at that job was short. I learned through the Antioch grapevine that there was a job opening at the Philadelphia Joint Board of the Amalgamated Clothing Workers Union that seemed to fit my interests more directly. The position offered to me was titled the Assistant Education Director and involved teaching classes for new members of the union and editing/writing the newspaper for the union. I wouldn't get rich working there but it provided me with a living wage. I started work at the union just as the 1960 presidential campaign was heating up and political possibilities permeated the union's agenda.

My experience there picked up on the interests I had honed at Antioch. The members of the Philadelphia branch of the union were predominantly women and people of color although the leadership of the union was drawn largely from white male communities (both Jewish and Italian). At the same time, there had been a strong tradition emphasizing the women's role in the Amalgamated's national organization that harked back to the concerns of the wife of the founder of the union. My boss at the Joint Board was one of a group of women in the labor movement who worked closely with Eleanor Roosevelt to provide educational opportunities for women union members. The union held summer schools in upstate New York near Mrs. Roosevelt's home. I was thrilled to attend those sessions and to meet Mrs. Roosevelt in her cottage near the family's Hyde Park site.

I discovered that one of the top officials of the union based in New York City was a distant relative of mine. When he found out that I was working at his union in Philadelphia he was amazed to learn that I had not used my family relationship as a way of getting the job. I realized that personal relationships were very important in job hunting but actually was proud to be able to say that I got the job on my own.

When I moved to Philadelphia I found an apartment in an area of the city called Powelton Village. Just a few blocks north of the University of Pennsylvania it was made up of houses built after the Civil War. The houses had originally been quite grand and the neighborhood's accessibility to trolley lines going to West Philadelphia had made it a choice residential spot for the city's industrial upper class. The houses were quite elegant, but by the 1920s the population had shifted and the area was populated by low-income families.

When I came to Philadelphia in the 1960s it was natural for an Antioch graduate to live in Powelton Village. The neighborhood was known as a multiracial area. It had a community organization that drew on relationships between the residents and those who worked at the Quaker American Friends Service Committee (headquartered in downtown Philadelphia). Some residents had relationships with the University, particularly those concerned about urban issues. Faculty and students from other colleges and universities found the neighborhood a compatible place. Both the anti-war demonstrations and early civil rights activity of the era involved residents from the area. The interracial environment in the community sometimes led to criticisms from some political and police groups in the city.

When the civil rights movement began in the South, it was not surprising that Powelton residents were involved in supporting those activities. A local chapter of the Congress of Racial Equality was organized and support for the sit-in movement in the South started regular demonstrations in the city. I learned about the complexity of organizing social change activities and finding a way to work out a shared agenda between a range of different participants with somewhat different goals. The CORE chapter first started supporting the sit-in activity by picketing the Woolworth's store in West Philadelphia. One day a young African American boy started to go into the store. We stopped him and gave him a quick lecture that tried to get him to understand why he shouldn't shop at Woolworth's. We finished our lecture. He looked up and said, "I don't shop. I steal." We sent him in.

After supporting the sit-ins in the South we then moved to more local issues (e.g. demonstrating against hiring patterns in Horn and Hardart's restaurant, sitting in a model house in a Northeast Philadelphia neighborhood). During that period I assumed that I would spend at least a part of every weekend in some protest activity. We were sensitive to our image and thus always tried to dress like respectable people, not like the hippies of the time. Our various demonstrations were almost always attended by FBI agents who were identifiable because they wore white shirts and business suits. They too were trying to be viewed as respectable citizens as they wore the uniform demanded by FBI head J. Edgar Hoover.

It was fortuitous that my job at the Amalgamated gave me the chance to connect my personal concerns and job responsibilities. It was appropriate in that setting to link my teaching responsibilities for new union members with my civil rights activities emanating from Powelton Village. I included articles on civil rights issues in the union newspaper, even receiving attention from the national Jewish Labor Committee for that coverage. My position in the union gave me a perspective on all kinds of activities within the Philadelphia liberal community. The social change that was taking place within the city was ignored by the daily press; it completely failed to cover the new civil rights organizations and activity. This realization provoked the leadership of the local Americans for Democratic Action organization to create a weekly newspaper that did include information on these types of activities. I soon found myself contributing articles to that weekly on a range of issues that otherwise would not have been covered in the printed press. It was a time of significant social change that was clearly related to political and intergroup activity. I was very pleased to be a part of that effort.

Up to that point, I used the Antioch job structure as the model for my expectations about work. Antioch jobs were likely to be less than a year in duration. While the Amalgamated job lasted about two years, it seemed to me that after two years it was time to move on. While I wanted to stay in Philadelphia, my interest in politics offered me a way to link my personal and professional agendas. I left the union and joined many of the same people I had worked with in the community as a staff member for a political campaign supporting U.S. Senator Joseph Clark for reelection and former Philadelphia mayor Richardson Dilworth for Pennsylvania governor. In that 1962 effort, Clark was reelected but Dilworth was defeated by the Republican candidate.

The Clark-Dilworth campaign showed me how it is not always easy to link one's personal and professional agendas. My knowledge of Philadelphia area civil rights issues was useful to the campaign and I was able to draw on my relationships with the civil rights community to involve them in the campaign. That evoked an unexpected reaction within the CORE community – at least unexpected to me. The Philadelphia CORE chapter saw itself as working outside of the establishment and felt that I was moving against that strategy. The CORE leaders called me in for what I came to call my CORE martial, chastising me for using my relationship within CORE for political gain. After the campaign was over I realized that I needed to separate my personal agenda from my work requirements. I spent nearly a year working at jobs that really didn't have much of a link to the social change I was committed to. I found that jobs that called on my writing skills provided that opportunity.

THE MARCH ON WASHINGTON

By the summer of 1963 civil rights activities across the nation were provoking concern at the national level. The August 28, 1963 March on Washington became the centerpiece for a broad range of groups that were pushing the Kennedy Administration to take action protecting African Americans in many different settings. The agenda involved jobs, public accommodation, and a range of legal approaches to desegregation. There was no way that I would miss that demonstration, joining civil rights advocates from religious, labor union, and other groups advocating passage of what became the 1964 Civil Rights Act. I was proud that

American Jews were visibly involved in the movement and its leadership.

That August day was incredible. Often described as more like a Sunday School picnic than the tense setting of demonstrations in the southern states, I spent the day walking around the area around the Lincoln Memorial observing the range of people among the 250,000 estimated to be in attendance. It was amazing to see the impact of the MLK "I Have a Dream" speech on the interracial audience drawn from multiple generations and people with very different experiences. For those of us who had been active in civil rights activities, the program speakers communicated the commitment to change that we had tried to evoke in our own work.

After the program was completed I walked around the Reflecting Pool with a friend and watched the organizers of the event quickly and efficiently pick up the trash from that huge group of people. There had been real concerns that the March would evoke violence. The daily press warned people about those dangers. But I always thought that taking the responsibility for cleanup showed how far that was from reality.

By the time the march took place I had already moved my attention away from issues in a single city to think about the civil rights movement in national terms. Strategizing about changes that would emanate from Washington meant that my personal focus would move in that direction. I had already linked my civil rights agenda to political processes; it now started to move to Washington.

MOVING TO WASHINGTON

I was able to draw on suggestions from several of my acquaintances to look for a job in Washington dealing with the growing national civil rights agenda. A conversation with a staff member at the U.S. Commission on Civil Rights uncovered a job possibility at the agency created by the passage of the 1957 Civil Rights Act. The job was the Assistant Information Officer at the Commission, working as an assistant to a very talented African American activist and poet who had recently moved to D.C. from Atlanta. M. Carl Holman was a faculty member at one of the predominantly Black Colleges there and had been an advisor to activist students from those colleges. The two of us enjoyed working with one another. I think I eventually convinced him that there were three groups of people involved in the civil rights issues: African Americans, Whites, and Jews.

Washington was beginning to be a magnet for individuals who shared a change agenda and there was a sense of possibility about change. At the time I came to the Commission a number of people my age were entering the federal government motivated by their commitment to the civil rights agenda. When the 1965 Voting Rights Act was being considered, a sizeable number of staff (particularly the younger staff) walked across the street to demonstrate in favor of the Act in front of the White House. They did that after work hours to separate their official and personal roles. Although I stayed at the Civil Rights Commission for only two years, that experience played a significant role in my future career development.

I had arrived in Washington on Friday, November 22, 1963, having driven from Philadelphia that day and planning to meet my moving van a few days later to move into the apartment I had rented. I remember that I was driving on US 95 for the first time since the highway had not been open very long. En route I noticed the first bumper sticker that called for the reelection of the Kennedy-Johnson ticket in 1964.

But that was not to be. By the time I pulled up to the front of my new apartment building the staff came up to me and said, "The president has died." I didn't know what they were talking about. Was it the president of the company that owned the apartment? Despite my focus on politics, I didn't ever think that they were referring to John Kennedy. I soon learned otherwise. I was coming to Washington to work for Kennedy and couldn't imagine what would develop in the future with his death. I was both mourning the country's loss as well as my personal loss and the uncertainties that would flow from this horrible death.

The next few days in Washington were surreal. Luckily I had close friends living near Capitol Hill and could join them. Some of us spent all night during the weekend standing in line at the Capitol to pay homage to Kennedy's body. People couldn't stop talking to each other. Strangers became friends in that line.

I was in the crowd waiting for the funeral procession to pass when we heard on the radio that Lee Harvey Oswald was shot in the Dallas police station by Jack Ruby. We all thought: what can happen next? The grandmother of one of my friends told us about her memories of the assassination of President McKinley in 1901. I vacillated back and forth between mundane tasks related to moving in and, at the same time, the larger than life issues that were associated with the assassination of a president.

When I started going to work the next week I tried to find some way to adapt to working in a government bureaucracy. I wasn't sure how to adapt to this new environment. By the beginning of the new year there were a number of new, younger staff in the organization. Most, however, were lawyers (as was the norm at the Commission). I didn't have many "natural" colleagues in the organization. Soon after I arrived a group of CORE members from the Washington CORE chapter sat-in at the Commission to protest a policy issue. That was confusing for me. These were individuals I knew but I was now on the inside of the issue, not on the outside (where I had been involved for the past several years).

During the time I was on the Commission staff I had a number of interesting responsibilities. I was a liaison to some of the journalists mostly from the print press who were assigned to cover civil rights issues. I helped put together a film of a Commission hearing in Mississippi. I wasn't allowed to attend the hearing because I was literally told, "You don't know how to behave in a segregated setting." But I vicariously attended because I watched hours and hours of footage from that hearing and made it into a film. I worked on various Commission reports and after the 1964 Civil Rights Act was passed, focused on efforts aimed at implementing Title VI of the Act – the requirement that federal funds should not be used to support segregation.

Because there were so many new people on the staff, the Commission organized a series of briefings by people from other federal programs and agencies, providing us with background information on what they were doing that was relevant to the Commission's agenda. My favorite briefings came from FBI staff who wanted us to know what they were doing. My knowledge of past efforts made me somewhat cynical about the FBI role, particularly in small southern towns where the FBI agents did not intervene when local law enforcement officials were violating the rights of African Americans.

One such event occurred in Americus, Georgia. The FBI agent who was the liaison to the Commission completed his briefing and then asked for questions. I asked him why the FBI agents in Americus did not stop the actions of the local law enforcement. When I completed my comments he asked me my name. I said, "Mary Smith." Everyone in the room laughed. The next day the FBI agent was in the Commission building and we crossed paths. He looked up and said, "Hi Mary."

I was also fascinated by the structure and culture of the federal government. While the Commission had a fairly unique mission and role, it was required to operate within the confines of the generic federal government requirements. I was amazed at some of those requirements. One day I was fighting a cold and needed to have hot water for tea available to drink to minimize my symptoms. My boss had a pitcher for hot water in his office and he suggested that I take that pitcher into my office. Within minutes the staff member responsible for personnel issues at the Commission marched into my office and said that I wasn't allowed to have that pitcher. It seems that every Government Service grade (at the time) was assigned specific items that were viewed as appropriate for the status of that grade. That included size of desks, tables, and miscellaneous items. And hot water pitchers weren't appropriate for someone of my grade. I subsequently found out that these lists were eventually eliminated by the Office of Personnel Management.

I was told by a friend that it is helpful to think of Washington, D.C. as a company town. And the company was the federal government. It is very difficult to disentangle politics and intrigue from the day-to-day operations of the city. When political parties change their status (from majority to minority) that shift permeated across the city. One of the large department stores in the city was known to change the style and type of items in their store windows when the administration changed. This was especially noticeable in the women's wear windows. I was quite familiar with the city since I had lived there for a few months on one of my Antioch jobs. I didn't realize that my return to D.C. started a pattern that was repeated into the 21st century: going to D.C. but then leaving D.C. for another location.

LEAVING THE COMMISSION

My two-year job cycle was coming to an end when several individuals from Britain came into the Commission office to discuss the development of a civil rights movement in the UK. Race relations were closely tied to issues related to the influx of immigrants into the country (many of them from the British empire who had British passports). At the time I was becoming more conscious of my limited experience beyond the U.S. My conversation with those individuals morphed into a plan to spend time in Britain working with research organizations and others concerned about government policies dealing with those immigrants. Even though the immigrants were formally "legal," issues of race and class created conditions not unlike those in the U.S.

My conversation led to a fairly detailed agenda for a trip. Not only would I be linked to the work of the National Committee for Commonwealth Immigrants (headed by the Archbishop of Canterbury), but I was also involved in the work of the Institute of Race Relations, particularly its Survey of Race Relations in Britain. I was assigned a project examining the general subject of British trade unions and what were termed "coloured immigrants." In addition, my British colleagues were among the leaders of an advocacy group called CARD – the Campaign Against Racial Discrimination. If that were not enough, they arranged for me to rent a room in the house of friends in the area of London called Canonbury for a modest amount. While I would receive some payment for my work, I decided that I would stay in the UK as long as my savings allowed. That turned out to be nearly a year. But within that year I not only learned an incredible amount through interviews with immigrant groups and trade unions but also managed to travel in Europe (that year included my time in the Soviet Union and Poland, Israel, Greece, Holland and much of the UK.)

It was fascinating for me to see how the political culture of Britain led to different responses to issues that were also found in the U.S. This was especially clear in the approach of trade unions to race issues. I found that the unions who identified their ideology as left wing (read Marxists) were likely to argue that the problems faced by the immigrants were created by class problems, not by race.

I had no idea what I would do when I returned to the U.S. I had developed a number of contacts in the U.S. in organizations that were experiencing budget limits that did not allow them to hire full time staff. As a result, I found it fairly easy to develop short-term projects with a range of labor union, poverty-related, and civil rights groups in town. In a sense, I was continuing the work structure that I had devised in London. I was somewhat embarrassed to call myself a "consultant," especially since I was often told that the term was a way of acknowledging that one was unemployed. I learned to work at home and to live modestly on the income I was able to develop.

But things rarely stand still and 1968 was an extraordinary year in the U.S. Civil rights issues were the subject of political debates, both in general and within the political system. Martin Luther King and Robert Kennedy were both assassinated, leaving the Democratic Party and the civil rights movement in shambles. The left had been split between supporters of Robert Kennedy and Eugene McCarthy; with Kennedy's death it wasn't clear whether Hubert Humphrey would be able to garner Kennedy's support.

The morning after the November 1968 election was a very gray and depressing day. I was walking around my neighborhood with a friend and acknowledged that I had no desire to stay in Washington when Nixon was in the White House. The realities seemed somewhat similar to my entrance in Washington in November 1963: Did I really want to be in the company town? What were my options?

CHAPTER 10

Crafting a Career: Discovering Academia

I did two things the morning after the 1968 election. I renewed my passport and I applied for a PhD program at the University of California at Berkeley. In career terms, I decided that it was time for me to return to school and pursue a PhD. I found the least structured program I could and it was at the University of California at Berkeley. The program was called Social Policies Planning and was located in the Department of City and Regional Planning. At the time I applied to Berkeley I learned that there were conversations about creating a public policy school. But it didn't officially open until my second year on campus.

As someone who graduated from Antioch College it wasn't surprising that I had begun my work experience by focusing on action in the world and specifically on social change. My four years at Antioch were influenced by the work of John Dewey and by Arthur Morgan, the man who revived the Antioch edge in higher education (and went on to be the first director of the New Deal agency, the TVA). The Antioch work-study structure emphasized the importance of learning from the world of practice. At the same time, the school lured its graduates to further their education and produced one of the highest percentages of graduates who went on to get PhDs.

I wanted to get a PhD for two reasons. First, I was tired of being the second person on projects and thought that the PhD degree would give me some status. I didn't really think about becoming an academic. And second, and perhaps most importantly, I wanted to use the incredible resources at Berkeley to try to figure out why the civil rights agenda that had been enacted through the Civil Rights Act of 1964 was not producing the results that I expected. I was particularly concerned about why Title VI of the Act (the section that prohibited discrimination in the use of federal funds) was not producing the results that I, and many others, expected. It was a very turbulent time and there was very little in my experience that allowed me to figure out what was happening. At that point the term "implementation" was not in the vocabulary of anyone either inside government or outside.

My quest for figuring out what was happening when new policies were being implemented was repeated in many policy areas. Both politicians and advocates – and eventually the academic community – focused on what was viewed as a failure of the 1960 era Great Society programs. Programs in education, poverty, labor, economic development, health and other domestic policy areas had not delivered on their promises. People like me tried to understand why the programs that had received strong political backing were not achieving the expected results. The Berkeley program allowed me to define my coursework with minimal requirements. I shopped for faculty and courses all over the university and enrolled in courses in political science, sociology, law, public policy, and city and regional planning. The combination of courses reflected viewpoints from both within and outside the system.

Berkeley was the academic place to be if one was concerned about the effectiveness of relatively new federal programs. The Berkeley Public Policy graduate program was in its design phase and Aaron Wildavsky – the first dean – put together something called The Oakland Project where various PhD students used the laboratory of Berkeley's neighbor, Oakland, to study the policy process at a local level. I'm not sure where the term "implementation" came from – but Wildavsky's co-authored book *Implementation* was one of the most fruitful results of the Oakland Project. Among the faculty at the policy program was Robert Biller, a graduate of the USC School of Public Administration, and my guru in all things organizational.

Although Berkeley was quite a different environment than my

previous educational experiences, it did provide me with a setting that captured my concerns. My colleagues in the program included a diverse array of people. Some came straight out of undergraduate programs and others (like me) came with significant work experience as their point of departure. Most of the people in the program were attracted to a new academic program that drew its intellectual identity from multiple disciplines and sought to find ways to link theory and practice. I certainly discovered that there were rich sources of theories that would help me understand the reasons why my expectations for implementation of Title VI had not materialized. Drawing faculty from across campus also sensitized me to the differences between fields and programs. Interestingly, our program was funded by the National Institute of Mental Health and sought to produce people who would be able to act as change agents in policy areas affecting mental health issues. At that point, those policy areas reached broadly to include housing, social services, education, health, criminal justice and other fields.

It was impossible to avoid soaking up the unique Berkeley culture and environment. About two weeks after I arrived and moved in I was sitting in my living room when a rattle occurred and items started falling off of my bookshelves. That was the first of my earthquake experiences and it provoked my comment, "Chicken Little: the sky is falling." During those first months I learned to read earthquake signals and to find a way to live through what was essentially forty days and forty nights of rain.

Demonstrations and other concerns dealing with the Viet Nam war also marked my time in Berkeley in the early 1970s. These occurred both on campus and in town. It was rumored that there had been so much tear gas released on campus that the trees there had learned how to adapt to it and use it as fertilizer. The political issues dealing with the war provoked both students and faculty to ask questions about the value of a range of traditional graduate program requirements (such as PhD exams) in an environment characterized by massive military expenditures and loss of life as a result of the war.

While these were not new issues for me, there was clearly a different way of dealing with them in the Berkeley setting. As a result, I learned to appreciate the differences between life on the west coast and that on the east coast and began a tradition of finding a way to spend some time in Berkeley throughout coming years. During my two years in residence in the Berkeley PhD program, I came to love the Bay Area environment and became quite familiar with the northern California region.

After meeting the formal course and exam requirements for the PhD, I focused on my dissertation. I followed through with my original intentions related to returning to school and focused on problems with implementation of civil rights requirements in the federal government as the subject of the dissertation. I had managed to explore pieces of that subject in various courses and was ready to embark on the final requirement for the doctorate. That started as an oral exam focusing on my dissertation proposal. I wasn't completely secure about how to deal with the oral exam but several friends recommended that I think about it as a ritual. I decided that I should use my personal experience with rituals as a way to deal with this new academic anxiety. Thus my preparation for the exam not only included my substantive academic work but I drew on my familiarity with rituals from my Jewish background. I brought wine, chopped liver and crackers for the four or five faculty on the committee. The faculty group sent me out of the room and I waited for them to call me back to discuss the substantive issues. After what seemed to me to be an eternity before that happened, I was called back and informed that I had passed the orals (without any discussion) and we would use the rest of the time to discuss my plans for completing the work. After we completed the discussion, I asked one of the faculty members why it took so long to bring me back in. He responded, "We were busy eating." As a result, providing food and drink at the orals became a regular practice in my department.

MOVING TOWARD THE ACADEMIC TRACK

I returned to Washington to do the research for my dissertation and found myself teaching full time for a year in the political science department at Goucher College outside of Baltimore. I was able to continue with my dissertation interviews in Washington and begin actually writing the dissertation when the Goucher job offer emerged. I replaced a faculty member who was on sabbatical (who eventually became a close friend and colleague.) This opportunity was surprising to me. Other than teaching new member courses at the union, I had never taught and frankly did not consider that to be my career path. During the year I taught six different undergraduate courses; that made me realize that teaching was something I could consider.

My next move continued my pattern of responding to opportunities that emerged. One of my Goucher students was applying for a master's degree at the LBJ School of Public Affairs at the University of Texas at Austin and told me about the program. Both of us landed there. I visited the LBJ School in November for an interview and during that visit was thrust in a social setting that continued the reach of the Johnson administration. Given my anti-war activity I did not consider myself to be a Johnson fan and wasn't sure that the LBJ school was somewhere I wanted to be. I discovered a fellow Antioch graduate on the law school faculty and found myself in a group of activist Texas liberals who were clearly in the minority in the political structure and were among the anti-Johnson residents. This was also before Austin became a trendy place to live.

The LBJ School was in its first years of operation and the faculty was still quite small. And, as I have noted, it was entirely male in composition. Like Antioch, the program linked theory and practice and students were required to develop policy research projects with actual clients and realistic decision-making settings. The structure of these projects allowed students and faculty to work closely together and find ways to address the policy problems that framed the projects. I learned that it was possible to develop a personal research and publications agenda that presented my perspective in at least two ways – one was written for practitioners while the other was written for academicians. That dual form become a predictable way for me to package my research and allowed me to keep both academic and practitioner identities in focus.

I don't think I ever expected to live long term in Texas. Soon after

I arrived in Austin in August 1973, I tried to find a way to become a part of the community. Austin itself had multiple cultures within its population. Some residents were "good old boys" inside the infamous world of Texas politics. Some were African American and Hispanic residents who lived on the margins of the community and were faced with the legacy of racism. The Jewish population in the city was very diverse reflecting the differences between people associated with the university and those in other jobs. Still others identified with the Texas liberal population that later supported Ann Richards for Governor and read the *Texas Observer* paper.

Despite my appointment within the university, I was not likely to become a central part of the community. In some ways, living in Austin reminded me of my early life in South Dakota. While I could try to assimilate to the Texas culture, I would never quite fit into it. I attended the High Holiday services at the Hillel on campus and found it strange to hear Hebrew spoken with a Texas accent. And while I had some good colleagues at the LBJ School, as I have noted earlier, it wasn't easy to be an outspoken Jewish woman in an otherwise all male faculty.

Sometimes my experiences living in Austin verged on the ridiculous. I had purchased a new car when I came to town and had decided that I wanted something cheerful so I chose a bright orange car. No one told me that orange was the University of Texas football team's color. As a result, when I drove around town others assumed that I was a devout football fan like those fans who wore orange suits to the games. At times, other drivers responded to my symbols of annoyance by waving to me and giving me the "Hook 'em Horns" symbol. Talk about miscommunication!

After several years in Austin I realized that I was not likely to get tenure at the LBJ School. I did manage to last four years on the faculty, publish my dissertation as my first book, develop colleagues and actually found much of my teaching and work with students extremely rewarding. But I did find it difficult to reconcile my personal values and goals with the dominant Texas culture.

After four years at the LBJ School and a change of administration in Washington I came back to D.C. to work in the federal government through an Intergovernmental Personnel Act position. That program was a way for individuals working in non-government settings to have a temporary placement in the federal government. I spent most of the year working on a project for Joseph Califano, then Secretary of the Department of Health, Education and Welfare. That effort sought to review the policies and programs in the department and publish its findings in a report modeled after one done in the Department of Defense. While the project never saw the light of day, it did provide me with a wonderful vantage point to see the department as a whole and to gain an understanding of a very complex federal organization that was responsible for implementing more than 300 different programs. About three-fourths of the way through the year (when the Califano project was shelved) I moved over to the Office of Management and Budget in the White House to work on President Carter's Presidential Reorganization Project. And by that time, both as a result of my experience in the federal government and exposure to some public administration literature, thinking about teaching in a public administration program seemed to make sense.

USC IN WASHINGTON

During my years at Texas Bob Biller (my Berkeley organization guru) had returned to University of Southern California to become the dean of the School of Public Administration. So when I recognized that I wanted to stay in Washington and consulted Biller about possibilities, he told me about the USC Washington Public Affairs Center (WPAC). Early in my federal fellowship, I visited the USC outpost, met the small faculty and eventually accepted a position at the Center. When I joined the faculty the Center had moved to a building in downtown Washington, across the street from Ford's Theatre and next door to the building where Abraham Lincoln had died. It was also just down the street from the FBI building. A look-alike of Lincoln roamed the street and was available for photos by tourists in the front of that building.

When I started conversations with USC and WPAC about the possibility of joining the faculty in the fall of 1978 I had a general sense of the reputation of the USC School of Public Administration but didn't have much detail about it. It was one of the highly regarded public administration programs in the U.S. But in truth, I wasn't someone who identified myself as a public administration person. While I was concerned about implementing legislation and other policy forms, I saw the challenge there trying to find a way to make sure that policies were actually carried out in a way that reflected their substantive values. To me, the public administration field highlighted the processes of management and not their impact on substantive outcomes. That was in contrast to the field of public policy, which seemed to emphasize social change.

That move to Washington was the sixth time I lived in the nation's capital. It was clear by that point that I had a clear pattern of going to D.C., leaving D.C., and returning to the city. I had begun this pattern with my Antioch job, then went to work for the Civil Rights Commission, returned from Britain to work as a consultant in D.C., returned to D.C. to work on my dissertation, worked in HEW, and stayed on to accept a teaching position at the Washington Public Affairs Center of USC. And it was followed by several other instances where I left D.C. and then returned. I didn't expect the USC Washington position to provide a longer-term home for me that would allow me to depart from my previous short-term job pattern.

LEARNING FROM MY STUDENTS

Professors always learn from their students. But the special student body at WPAC made that experience richer than many programs. The diverse array of students in both the doctoral and master's degree classes at the Center gave me an unusual perspective on the Washington scene. I didn't have to depend on the *Washington Post's* Federal Diary column to learn what was occurring in the many organizations that make up the aggregate D.C. culture. Those students (particularly the doctoral students) were mid- to high-level careerists who brought experience and expertise to the classroom. There wasn't a hierarchical separation between faculty and students; many DPA students became good friends (and some friends actually became DPA students). I had some appreciation of the unique cultures of agencies but when those cultures came into the classroom, I learned more about them.

My personal experience had been in domestic social policy agencies so I was particularly struck by the cultures of other agencies. Conversations in classes were frequently punctuated with an array of abbreviations that some called alphabet soup (or a jumble of letters). I was known to accuse some Department of Defense staffers of speaking in code since I had a hard time figuring out what they were saying. It was difficult for me to hear FBI agents refer to women agents as "girl agents." When I started calling male agents "boy agents" I think my discomfort with gender stereotyping was understood. I had one class that included students from both the CIA and the FBI. They brought their agency policies and behaviors with them to the classroom. For example, all of them sought seats around the table but avoided having their backs to the door. That allowed them to see who was entering the room and also minimized visual access to the window. When I had classes that included staff from the FBI, Drug Enforcement Agency, and the Bureau of Prisons, I saw how the personnel policies of each of those agencies came alive in career patterns and even dress codes.

Clearly the structure of the DPA program provided opportunities for both students and faculty to appreciate individual differences between job settings and individual responses to those settings. The program was organized around an intensive semester; that format allowed students who were working fulltime to work around both their work and academic schedules. That format gave students their syllabus a month before the class met, provided them with reading and writing assignments, brought them to the Center for four days (nine to five), had additional assignments and a month later another four days of class, and then a final assignment. This format allowed students to organize their work around the class schedule if they had travel or other responsibilities. I sometimes described the intensive semester as akin to summer camp where participants created a bond that clearly lasted beyond the experience itself.

The most unique aspect of the doctoral program was the Autobiographical Learning Plan. It was the first class in the doctoral program and required students to undertake a highly personal writing project that would serve as the way to determine whether there was a fit between a student's goals and the abilities of the program to meet them. They would describe their life and career goals; undertake research among family, friends, and work associates to determine whether the fit was available; and establish a learning plan based on the data and insights they acquired in the process. Actually that document was a gold mine. I was always somewhat uncomfortable with the process of grading them since, in effect, one was grading another individual's life! And there were always surprises in the process of reading those documents. One army colonel discussed various options that might be available to him in terms of future career development. I almost fell out of my chair when I read that one option he was seriously considering involved becoming a male nurse (his term)! Not what one would expect, particularly during the late 1970s.

For years I had been opposed to the traditional dissertation defense process in most universities. I found it insensitive to schedule a defense when the faculty knew that the student wasn't ready to defend his or her work. It was strong evidence of the infantilization built into graduate education. My personal experience at Berkeley indicated that other modes of assessment were possible. So we didn't schedule a defense at the Washington Center unless the faculty thought that the student was likely to make a successful presentation. And I loved the celebration process that was structured in the DPA program with refreshments that moved beyond my wine and chopped liver experience at Berkeley.

DPA students provided me with access to opportunities that would have been difficult for me to gain on my own. One year I had a spring visit to the Army War College at the end of the yearlong program for individuals who were likely to be moving up the career ladder in the Army. That was an incredible experience for me. I learned so much about the inside of DoD and changed many of my views about the military. Similar shifts in my views occurred as a result of my exchange with students from the FBI and other agencies dealing with criminal justice. When doctoral students took some courses with master's students, both learned how important it was to reach beyond their organizational and generational realities. Often DPA students were amazed at perceptions by the master's degree students and those younger students loved to have contact with high level careerists. Each year that I spent at the Center built on my personal experience at the Civil Rights Commission when I too was a bureaucrat. While the Commission experience introduced me to one world of the federal bureaucrat, teaching at the USC Washington Center provided me with a real understanding of the complex and diverse dimensions of the federal government.

SIXTEEN YEARS AT WPAC

I stayed on the faculty of the Center for sixteen years. I found that the structure of the academic life allowed me to keep up with changes in the public sector through involvement with different groups of students, modifications in policies and organizations, changes in the relationship between the Washington Center and the home base in Los Angeles, and utilizing sabbatical leaves to explore policy and management issues in other countries. I developed knowledge of policy and public administration issues in both Australia and India. As a result, I finally departed from my pattern of short-term job experiences. I learned about the demands of running a small organization when I became the director of the Center. I knew about traditional functions attached to academic administration but the outpost nature of the Center called on the director to assume responsibility for many housekeeping requirements. No one had told me that the work of the Center could not be accomplished without an elevator that worked and a heating-air conditioning system that allowed people to sit in the classroom for hours upon end. In addition, we could have a revolution if we ran out of coffee and tea!

In some ways, running WPAC gave me a new perspective on some traditional management issues. My own research had dealt with tensions between field and headquarters organizational units. But when I had to live with that tension in the context of three-hour time differences and minimal authority at the field level, I understood this problem in new ways. We had to deal with Los Angeles headquarters for even small decisions. I saw that issues became more difficult – even polarized – when the players in the conversation did not have face-to-face contact. Until Skype and other technology allowed visual contact, I was convinced that the LA faculty would actually leave the room without telling us who was left, or what was actually occurring.

I also learned a lot about the politics of budgeting. I knew a bit about the academic literature on budgeting but I experienced it in a different way when dealing with constantly changing budget rules. Because the USC Washington Center was an integral and legal part of the Los Angeles based program it was dependent on decisions made by the majority of faculty on the other side of the country. As a result, year after year we would learn how to play the budget game and then, in the succeeding year, be confronted with a new system.

But perhaps I learned the most about the realities of higher education. It is very difficult to try to impose a new model on an entrenched system. Perhaps I should have expected this since I'm a student of implementation. But I wasn't prepared for the intense battles both in our faculty and in the profession itself between traditional PhD advocates and those of us who wanted to devise a different approach that would meet the needs of adult practitioners (called a Doctorate in Public Administration – a DPA). I think it is very difficult for an academic department to contain both of the degrees. When I was involved in professional committees on "doctoral" education, I tried very hard to identify those attributes that were found in both types of programs. Although public administration has always been an academic field directly influenced by the world of practice, the tension between theory and practice has never been avoided. Working out curriculum and program requirements has been problematic and tense, particularly when other structural and fiscal pressures are at play.

ANOTHER DEPARTURE FROM WASHINGTON

Staying at USC for sixteen years was surprising to me (and to many of my friends). I departed from my past pattern of coming to Washington and then finding a reason to leave after just a few years. It was especially surprising because of the political reality in Washington during those sixteen years from 1978 to 1994. While I continued to be involved in various activities that largely supported the Democratic Party, I did manage to find a home in the USC Washington Center that allowed me to maintain my own personal political activity as well as deal with academic norms of openness and fair mindedness. That was largely true during a period that encompassed the last half of the Carter administration, all eight years of Reagan's two terms, George H. W. Bush's term, and the first part of Clinton's administration.

As I approached my late fifties, it seemed to me that probably one more notch was yet to be made in my career belt. I was contacted by the search committee at the Rockefeller College of the SUNY Albany campus and asked if I would be interested in being considered as the chair of the Department of Public Administration and Policy within the College. At that point I was fairly visible within the broader public administration and policy fields and believed that my approach to those disciplines was less marginal than it had been earlier in my career. In addition, much of my research in that period involved federalism issues and the relationship between policies and programs at the federal and state levels. I was attracted to a position in the New York state capitol that would allow me to make some contrasts with life in the Texas state capitol of Austin. I decided to accept the Albany offer and gave myself more than a year and a half before I actually moved from Washington and USC. Leaving the Washington Center after sixteen years was fairly complex. Since I was the chair of ten doctoral dissertation committees I wanted to complete those responsibilities before I left. I was able to do that and gradually made my move to Albany.

Chairing the Albany department for nearly two years (1994-95) was more problematic than I had expected and it was particularly difficult for someone who was an outsider to the Department, the University, and the political environment. I was the first chair who came from outside the department. Albany itself had a distinct culture that combined New England behavior with behaviors very like those found in the Midwest. I did manage to join a small group of Jewish women from the university in a book group. That was something I didn't find in Austin or Aberdeen. And I probably misjudged the difference between the operations of a private university (USC) and a public institution. In some ways, the situation repeated some of my difficult experiences in Austin.

After a year it was clear to me that I really missed Washington and I recognized that I had a serious case of Potomac Fever (defined as a disease based on a desire to be close to the power of the U.S. Federal Government in Washington, D.C.). I found myself the owner of two houses – one in Washington that was being rented because the market for sales was not very healthy when I moved to Albany and the second in Albany that was significantly less expensive than my D.C. house. Once again I found a way to identify a refuge in Washington by utilizing the Intergovernmental Personnel Act, assuming a temporary position in the Clinton administration through the assistance of Secretary of Health and Human Services (HHS) Donna Shalala, a long time friend. I managed to move back to Washington, moved into my Washington house, and started a position in the Office of the Assistant Secretary for Management and Budget in HHS, working with the Assistant Secretary, John Callahan. That arrangement was a godsend. Not only did it mean that I was returning to Washington – my real "home" – but it provided me with an incredible position within the Department and allowed me to become a participant observer in a number of interesting policy and management initiatives. I was able to stay in that position for two years and developed observations and experiences that became an important part of my future research agenda. I was able to watch the Department implement the Government Performance and Results Act from the inside and observe the relationships between the various parts of the large, sprawling Department.

By that time, it was clear to my colleagues at Albany (and to me) that I wanted to live in Washington. The Dean of my Albany school came up with a solution: I would live in Washington but commute to Albany during the academic year, Monday through Wednesday. That would allow me to teach my two courses and with the advent of the Internet keep in touch with colleagues and students through available technology. I had a regular schedule: leaving home on Monday morning for D.C.'s National

Airport, coming into Albany before noon, checking into a local bed and breakfast, and walking to school where I had office hours and other responsibilities. My classes were usually held on Tuesdays – one during the morning and the other in the late afternoon. This worked effectively until the disaster on 9/11. It was surrealistic to be teaching that morning and learn about the plane crashes at ground zero. National Airport was closed for about a month and my flights to Albany were shifted from Baltimore, complicating the trip somewhat.

A MOVE TOWARD RETIREMENT

Despite this, I continued to commute until the end of 2001. At that point I found it difficult to maintain a life in both settings. I had assumed the editorship of a public management journal in 2000 and that further complicated my life in Albany. I also turned sixty-five and recognized that it would be easier for me to have a less complex schedule. I joined the public administration faculty at the University of Baltimore and moved the journal to that setting. Commuting from D.C. to Baltimore was somewhat easier; it involved either driving there or taking the commuter train. I continued editing the journal and also helped to create a doctoral program for practitioners in the Washington-Baltimore area. Since the USC program had closed by that time, I used my experience with that program as the basis for the Baltimore effort.

I stayed in Baltimore for four years before I moved to the School of Public Affairs at American University from 2005 to 2011. That move further eased my commuting schedule since it was only a few blocks from my residence. In addition, I decided that I was at a stage of life when I could accept a part-time appointment as a way of moving toward retirement. As I write this I have been an adjunct faculty member at the McCourt School of Public Policy at Georgetown University for nearly five years. I have taught classes in public management for the public policy graduate students (mostly straight out of undergraduate programs) and supervised capstone projects for practitioner students (many of whom are international students) who have enrolled in a yearlong master's program.

While my teaching role has diminished somewhat as I have moved from school to school, my research production has actually increased. I have written or edited eight books since moving to Albany. In addition, I have served as the editor of a book series on Public Management and Change published by Georgetown University Press that has published thirty books. I continue to try to link theory and practice believing that as the world changes, the field has to respond to new demands.

CHAPTER 11

Typewriters, Writing ... and Apple

There were many things in our household that were an important part of my childhood. But one of the most central items was my mother's typewriter. It probably was the original one that she brought back from New York City – an ancient portable Smith Corona that she pulled out to write letters and produce miscellaneous memos and lists. That machine was one that she was reluctant to share. I didn't know anyone else who had a mother who had a typewriter at home let alone one who treasured it. When I visited my father's office, I made a beeline for the office machines there (typewriters, adding machines). I was allowed to use those machines. But there was something different about my mother's typewriter.

Until I read the letters from my mother to my father written in the early months of their relationship, I wasn't conscious of the importance of the typewriter to my mother. Those letters told me – for the first time – that the typewriter had a special meaning to her. It was her link to her work life as well as her way of writing letters to people who were not available for face-to-face communication. I realized that writing (eventually with the aid of the typewriter) was something that she had excelled in since her high school days. And it was something that I have come to realize that I shared with her.

I don't think I have ever described myself as a writer yet it is clear to me that throughout my journey to develop a career my ability as a writer was something that I relied on. Over the years I used that skill in a number of different ways. But it was clearly something that became an essential part of my identity. And that it was a "something" I shared with my mother. Probably at some unconscious level the ability to type and write was related to my sense of independence and possibilities.

HOW I DEVELOPED MY WRITING SKILLS

One summer I took typing lessons and excelled in the class. My ability to play the piano probably contributed to that accomplishment; both built on my digital facility. When my brother Arthur's Bar Mitzvah came about, my Aunt Rose arrived to help my mother prepare for the festivities. Sensitive to the many gifts that my brother would receive (and I wouldn't) my aunt told me that she was giving me a typewriter as a combination gift for my next birthday and the next Hanukkah. Before the Bar Mitzvah event we picked out the portable typewriter – a Smith Corona portable model of the early 1950s. It was clear to my Aunt Rose that a typewriter represented something very meaningful to me and thus might counteract the jealousy I was likely to feel because Bat Mitzvah celebrations for girls weren't a part of the possibilities in the Aberdeen synagogue (although they were found in other synagogues).

From that time, a typewriter and its next generation – the computer – were the tools that allowed me to develop a set of skills that I was able to employ in very diverse settings. Like the piano, it was the vehicle that allowed me to express myself and to achieve a level of digital dexterity. The typewriter I received from my aunt accompanied me to college and was my instrument of choice almost until I discovered computers (a real office typewriter came into the picture in my house before computers). Writing became a way for me to communicate with others but also a way to influence the way that I was able to take action. The form of the writing changed over my career as I attempted to try out different approaches.

As I think about this pattern now, in some ways it does repeat the way that my mother used her typewriter. It was her way to reach out to people and to express her views. But I pushed it somewhat further than my mother. I saw a form of advocacy resulting from my writing.. It was not simply reporting information but it was trying to convince others to take action in a direction of my choice. Perhaps it was my way of being a salesperson like my father. This translated into a combination of journalism and promotion of an agenda.

JOURNALISM

By the time I graduated from high school I was likely to tell people (if pushed) that I was interested in becoming a journalist. One of my extracurricular activities in high school revolved around the school newspaper. I did not have a major role on the newspaper but was one of the staff members who could knock out a story rapidly and competently. I learned to organize my work responding to the classic "who, what, where and when" questions and was able to grasp elements of a situation very quickly. I also learned how to put a newspaper together in academic journalism classes. If I thought about future careers, it was probably journalism of some sort that structured my expectations.

Antioch provided me with opportunities to try out new things since I did not have a clear idea of what I wanted to do when I graduated. Because Antioch was constructed on an educational approach that combined work and study, when it came time for me to think about a work experience I was attracted to a job at the Washington, D.C. office of the Associated Press. It didn't involve writing but required me to take dictation – a highly stylized process in the organization where reporters who were out in the field phoned in their stories and someone at the other end typed them. Those typed versions were then given to the editor who moved the information along the distribution chain. It ended with a story that went out on the tickertape machine. I became one of those typists and my prowess as a fast typist who also seemed able to comprehend the substance of the story was valued.

The months that I spent working at the Associated Press included journalistic attention to major health problems of then President Eisenhower as well as a range of other classic Washington stories. The reporters liked to chat with me (amused by a 19 year old woman who was very enthusiastic about their work) and were willing to let me accompany them to press conferences when I wasn't working. I also was able to attend congressional hearings. The most memorable hearing was before the House UnAmerican Activities Committee when African American singer Paul Robeson was brought before hostile members of Congress and refused to accept their views of citizenship.

My hours at the job were not based on a traditional business schedule and I usually worked on weekends, allowing me to have time off during the work week. It was great for me to get to meet with well-known reporters whose by-lines were familiar to me as a newspaper junkie. Two years later I had another Antioch job at the United Nations in New York. My job was to write captions for photographs that were used along with press releases in the UN Secretariat structure. In that job I was able to do more than type! But my activist urges were not satisfied by a traditional journalist role. Not only was I intrigued by decision-making and the world of national politics but I also caught Potomac fever.

As I look back at those early stages of my career it does seem that I was exploring quite different approaches to a journalist's role. At least five different roles were beginning to take form. First, I saw the journalist and the press as a watchdog of government activity. Second, I saw the journalist and the press as an advocate for important views that were not emerging from traditional sources. Third, I saw the role of the journalist as a way to provide a voice for citizens, particularly those who lacked power and influence in the society. Fourth, I saw the journalist and the press as a translator of formal policy to the general public. And fifth, I saw the role of the journalist and the press as a way of demystifying official information in a way, which encouraged citizens to criticize the formal pronouncements. There were elements of each of these in the jobs I held in the coming years but all of them reflected a combination of writing and policy action.

When I returned to Antioch after my AP job I took a job as the Assistant Community Manager of the Antioch community. Antioch was one of the earliest institutions of higher education to create a decision-making structure that gave students an important role in governance. But I wasn't ready to give up journalism and thus for months I not only sat at the decision-making table in my official role but I also covered the meetings for the college newspaper. There were times when the two roles were in conflict but I wasn't ready to give up either one of them. I was trying to wear several hats at once and sought a way to focus on the multiple uses of the written word. I did not want to settle on a single role.

I still had some ideas about a journalism career and symbolically took rolls of tickertape paper back to Antioch from the AP. This was the paper that was used in tickertape machines in every newspaper around the country. I used the paper roll to write drafts of papers for my classes and often described my progress on the assignments not in number of pages but in the length of the roll (the number of feet completed) since I kept the roll going in one long piece. Inserting that paper roll into the typewriter gave me the sense that I was somehow linked to the newspaper world.

WRITING AS ADVOCACY OR ANALYSIS?

When I finished my Bachelor's degree at Antioch I wasn't sure what I wanted to do. I had been a history major but it was really a generic liberal arts experience that could move in multiple directions. I decided to continue my education and enrolled in a master's degree in American Studies at the University of Minnesota. Rather than narrow my career options that program actually broadened them. Not only did I take courses in American history and political science but I also took courses in art history, music and literature. While this was a very interesting graduate program, it did not fit a model of specialization in a specific academic field that most people I knew chose. My production of academic papers was very diverse and the assignments exposed me to a wide range of possibilities. The aggregate of my written work represents elements of all of the five roles I have identified.

My move to Philadelphia and the job at the Amalgamated Clothing Workers Union allowed me to combine my interest in journalism and advocacy. Writing and the written word were important to me both on their own intrinsic merits but also because they were linked to substantive policy agendas. Writing for *The Pennsylvania Guardian* allowed me to regularly write articles on civil rights issues and other related topics.

My jobs following the Amalgamated experience continued to reflect my combined strategy linking writing and policy action. I was hired to put out a newspaper for a group challenging the leadership of a Teamsters Union local on the waterfront. The group was called the Voice of the Teamsters and its members answered the phone, "This is de Voice." I was taken to a church along the waterfront where the Voice was meeting. The people I was working with wanted me to get a sense of the dynamics of this union battle but I was warned that women were not really welcome at the meeting. So I was hidden in the place where the organist sat during church where I could not be seen. The tension in the church was obvious and I was eventually smuggled out of the meeting. I learned that several Voice members were beaten up on their way home that evening. But I learned a lot about the dynamics of the union election process as I put out the newspaper.

ACADEMIC WRITING

My transition to the academic world really began with my dissertation. Back in the days before personal computers were widely available, one of the major concerns for would-be academics was the process that they would use to produce their ticket for their future: the dissertation. In the early 1970s that process was very messy. It involved lots of cutting and pasting of typed changes to the document that resulted from comments from the dissertation committee as well as modifications made by the hopeful PhD student him or herself. Because I was physically located in Washington, D.C. and two-thirds of my committee was in Berkeley, the process became even more difficult. In addition, the dissertation pages were supposed to be totally accurate and if typos were found, the page itself had to be retyped. It was not possible to use White Out to change a word or two.

When it was time for me to complete the dissertation I flew to Berkeley with a draft that would go to the typist (a person known for her accuracy) and returned to Washington with four copies of the final version that would be sent to the committee members. I had read horror stories about PhD students losing their dissertations on the New York subway so I carried two copies with me on the plane and packed two copies separately in two different suitcases. All copies arrived safely and my degree followed.

The mechanics of completing my dissertation almost seemed to overwhelm the substantive elements involved in the process. There were a number of elements in the process that reflected the chaos of the Berkeley environment I was experiencing. My academic program was intensely interdisciplinary and reflected my tendency to link often separate academic fields together. That provided me with latitude in the way I approached the task. This was a moment in time when there was not strong agreement on the methodology to be used for a doctoral dissertation in my field and, instead, faculty members were often willing to defer to the student's choice. I often thought of my dissertation committee as a decision-making body that had its own set of political relationships. So my task was to devise a document that would pass muster with all the members of the committee. Because I had arrived at Berkeley with a fair amount of knowledge about the topic of the dissertation there seemed to be a tendency for the committee members to give me latitude to proceed. I knew where to find appropriate documents in the Archives and had personal knowledge as well as access to many of the officials who were willing to have me interview them about the issue.

In addition, the intellectual climate in the public policy field was in a period of change and growth. New academic programs were established and new journals began to emerge. At that point, debates about the field often included both academics and practitioners and resulted in arguments about whether the subject to be studied was best described as an art or a science.

Once I completed the dissertation, I went on the market for an academic job. As a result, I spent four years in Austin, Texas as an academic. While life in Austin wasn't always comfortable, in other ways the LBJ School was very compatible with my concerns. It focused on policy issues that were relevant. Both my colleagues and many of my students emphasized the importance of developing policy research approaches that were multi-disciplinary and focused on the needs of real decision makers. The reports that emerged from joint faculty-student research processes showed me that collective writing could be creative and able to express multiple perspectives on the increasingly complex policy problems. This was eye opening to me since I had assumed that writing was a solitary activity. It started me on a path of turning out publications that were jointly authored.

As I have noted earlier, I did not last long at the LBJ School and actually found ways to leave Austin during summers, often involved in consulting in a practitioner environment. I found that there were many attributes in the Austin environment that reminded me of some of my negative experiences growing up in Aberdeen. My outspoken advocacy of racial and gender issues did not find a comfortable home in Austin. But despite this, from that point on I decided that the combination of teaching and writing was the pathway I would take. And the classic criteria used to evaluate an academic – teaching, publication, and service – seemed to be appropriate for me. At the same time, I was convinced that I could continue to be involved in both the academic and practitioner worlds.

That was clear when I returned to Washington to spend a year in the federal government as a staff person assigned to work on a project in the Office of the Assistant Secretary for Planning and Evaluation in the Department of Health, Education and Welfare. The assignment involved participating with a group developing a report covering policies affecting the entire department. While I spent most of the year on that project (which was never completed because of very relevant political issues that kept the report out of circulation) I also spent several months working in the White House Office of Management and Budget on the president's reorganization project. Both of these assignments gave me some sense that it was possible to combine academic work with the world of practice. Public administration at the time was a field that valued both the academic and the practitioner perspective on the role and activity of the public sector. I later learned to call myself a "pracademic" since I valued working in both settings.

WHAT ABOUT WRITING?

My writing tool at the LBJ School was a traditional typewriter. Soon after I arrived at the USC Washington Center there were intimations that a new tool would be available to the faculty – the computer. But I found it very difficult to comprehend the possibilities that seemed to be attached to that technology and relied on my research assistants to use it and move in its direction. Despite my attraction to typewriters, I identified myself as a 20th century Luddite – someone who was like the 19th century English textile workers who protested against new machinery. Because of this view, I feared that I would be stuck in the typewriter technology forever. I thought of myself as akin to those people I knew who reverted to a quill pen in their writing efforts.

I tried and tried to find a way to avoid that. I was working on a book and decided to go to the Eastern Shore beach for a week between Christmas and New Year's to make progress on the book project. I drove to the beach in the mid 1980s with several boxes of books and articles as well as a Kaypro computer. The Kaypro was one of the earliest portable computers; it weighed approximately 30 pounds and was large and very bulky. I had rented a studio apartment that overlooked the ocean and I dragged the dining room table to the window thinking that if I moved the computer to the table my view of the water would inspire me. While I was fairly productive during that week, I still was not comfortable with computers and continued to call myself a Luddite.

All of this changed a few years later when I went to the Australian National University in Canberra, Australia for my sabbatical semester. I arrived at the ANU and was immediately provided with one of the early Macintosh Computers devised by Apple's legendary Steve Jobs. I had never seen a Macintosh before and was expecting to respond to it as I had to the IBMs and other personal computers that were available to me. I was shocked. I recognized that that cute little box had a brain that was similar to mine. Both of us were right brained. It processed information by scanning it and not focusing on details. It emphasized visual images and reached for the big picture. I realized that my problem with some computers was not that they were machines but they were machines that assumed the users saw the world in linear terms. It was never clear to me how the Australian National University had moved to become an Apple devotee. On subsequent trips I found that the Apple products were replaced by PCs because the higher cost of the Apple products had pushed the University to change their products and purchase PCs.

From that time on, I became an avid Apple customer. I didn't care that no one else I knew at that time had a Mac and that the Apple products were more expensive than others. My mode of thought and the Apple machines were extremely compatible. I don't know how many Macintoshes I have owned since that time but every few years I have upgraded a desktop computer and added laptops, phones and iPads to my collection. At first, it was difficult to work with others when most of my potential colleagues were using PCs. When Microsoft developed software for both PCs and Apples, I found that I could write collaboratively with many different people. It didn't matter what continent my collaborators lived in. The technology allowed us to work together. In a sense that was my first real acknowledgement of globalization.

Yet most of the universities I have worked in were reluctant to acknowledge the strengths of Apple products. Almost every university and college had IT offices populated by staff who were convinced that the Apple products were fly-by-night merchandise. It is just relatively recently that the IT staff in higher education have acknowledged that they have to be prepared to trouble shoot non-PC technology. This is particularly ironic since every campus I know has a large number of students who have purchased and use Apple products. Watching the students sit on the hall floors or in other non-classroom settings with their Apple laptop computers does give new definition to the term "Apple orchard."

It was difficult to convince a range of academic institutions and public sector organizations that not only graphic designers want Apple products. I became computer ambidextrous with Apple products at home and PCs in my office. I was known for yelling at those PCs and constantly asking why couldn't they be more like Apples. My advocacy of the range of Apple products wasn't expected of someone of my age or role. I loved it when students and children of my friends pronounced that I was "with it" for someone of my background and age. When I was growing up I used to belittle my mother for running to the encyclopedia to check on information related to a conversation. A few years ago I realized that I was doing the same thing with my iPhone. But I use Google rather than the encyclopedia to access relevant information very quickly. It is certainly less cumbersome (and probably few people have volumes of encyclopedias accessible to them anymore).

There was a substantive product of my attachment to Apple. The iPhone allowed me to work closely with individuals across the globe without paying high telephone charges. It was possible to write a book with seven co-authors (not an edited volume) because we could edit each other's work easily. When that book appeared on Amazon, it was difficult for Amazon to acknowledge that there were actually seven authors for the work. Two authors might be acknowledged but seven didn't seem possible and clearly cumbersome. But it actually can occur.

In the 1970s I often commented that the Cuisinart food processor had changed my life. But by the 1980s that comment was superseded by the impact of the Apple computer on my world. Beyond its role assisting communication within the academic community, it also provided me a way to stay in touch with the world of practitioners. The gulf between theory and practice was narrowed when comments could be developed that were up to date and very topical rather than waiting for publication in academic journals or books.

We know that journalism has changed dramatically because of its constant ability to respond to breaking news and to find information at the drop of a hat. The same thing has happened to the academically produced written word. No longer is there a rigid distinction between the worlds that must move between cultures and time zones. We can thank computer technology for much of that.

ACADEMIC EXPECTATIONS SHIFT

In many ways it was a gift to me to be protected at the USC Washington Center at a time of changes in my academic fields of public administration and public policy. That meant that the criteria used in tenure and promotion decisions were flexible enough at that time to allow me to continue on the "pracademic" pathway (the combination of both practitioner and academic roles). But as time went on, these academic fields were moving toward defining the field as a science rather than an art. My interest in the practice of the fields of public administration and public policy led me to believe that some processes automatically resist definition and standardization. Different contexts are likely to generate different solutions to difficult problems. Interviews with practitioners at all levels of an organization provide incredible insight about the realities they are experiencing. That allowed me to use both top-down and bottom-up sources of information. Thus it is important to examine those processes in action and use those insights to define new solutions. In contrast, the advocates of defining the fields as science were more likely to focus on deductive processes that began with theoretical views and sought information "in the real world" that would support or contradict those theories.

My motivation for research led me to find ways to develop research projects in areas that often lacked formal data systems or were in the midst of change. Like many others in the past, that experience brought me to appreciate the traditional dichotomy between politics and administration. That tension between the two approaches was something that I had always recognized in my personal activities but came to appreciate in a more systematic way. That became an important theme in my written work.

As a result, I was inspired to write in new forms; several of my books have attempted to integrate traditional academic presentations with fictional characters that I presented as individuals who must deal with the relevant issues analyzed. This approach seemed especially effective for books that are written for classroom use. My book on the development of the policy analysis field illustrated the changes in the field through the use of three different people who used different approaches to the profession. While these individuals were fictional they are usually based on a real person (or persons) or real situations. One such person accosted me at a meeting proclaiming that he wasn't the fictional person I had created. I assured him that he wasn't. But he was right. His career was reflected in that fictional character. I found that these fictional characters were especially effective with students (students who were both pre service and practitioners) who are often in graduate programs aimed at training practitioners. This approach has tended to humanize often theoretical and abstract approaches. Perhaps most importantly, it made it possible for people with different backgrounds to be open to change.

About fifteen years ago I discovered another aspect of writing. I became the managing editor of a relatively new journal in the public management field. I found this role to be stimulating. It provided me with an opportunity to encourage people to utilize a range of methodologies and deal with a variety of issues that often were not used or examined. The journal jumped in status/ranking in the five years I served as editor and a yearly award for the best paper in the publication was named after me. As time has gone by, however, that journal (like a number of others) has published articles almost exclusively using quantitative analysis methods and has tended to avoid work that employs qualitative and theoretical approaches.

When that experience concluded, I convinced the Georgetown University Press to establish a book series dealing with public management and change. The series is the largest collection of books in a single series in this field. While written for use in the American classroom, these books have also been able to draw an audience of practitioners and individual faculty members across the globe. The authors of works in this series have been a mixture of established scholars and younger scholars (many of whom are women).

AM I A WRITER?

Over the years I have learned that one can use writing skills in a variety of ways. Many of the issues that I have been concerned with are embedded in important value conflicts. They deal with differences in needs and expectations of different population groups. The structure of American federalism makes it difficult to develop policies that meet that range of expectations. In that context, neutral views about information are often limited and difficult to determine. While the academic world often presents itself as composed of objective and detached observers, many of the issues that emerge from the policy and public administration field are embedded in a range of values. The stereotype of the cynical journalist who just tells it like it is has limited application to many of the issues I have examined. The five writer roles that I identified early in my career are also found in my motivations for academic research. As an author I too have served as a watchdog of government activity, an advocate for important views that were not emerging from traditional sources, a voice for citizens, a translator of formal policy to the general public, and a source of demystifying information from officialdom that allowed citizens to criticize the formal pronouncements. It has been important for me to be able to utilize writing in a way that links theory and practice and allows me to transcend the too common separation between advocacy and analysis.

CHAPTER 12
The Problem of Categories

When I was a child I enjoyed playing 52 Pickup. That's the children's card game that used a standard deck of fifty-two playing cards and is usually played as a practical joke. It is a tactic employed by someone who might be losing a card game as a disruption to that game. Usually my brother was the victim of my decision to gather all the cards on the table and in my hand and throw them on the floor. The only way to determine whether all of the fifty-two cards had been recovered was to arrange them either by suite or by number. That is, to establish the categories and start a new game.

But my interest in that process did not focus on finding a way to establish those categories. Rather, it was my fascination with disruption and complexity and stirring up expectations about what would happen next. There are clearly others who think that this response was not positive. But I seem to have thrived in that uncertainty. My tendency to stay at a job for a limited time (with the exception of the years at the USC Washington Center) reflected that personal predilection. I discovered still another approach to this tendency when I lived in northern California. Visiting the Winchester Mystery House I observed an example of a way to express my tendency to seek uncertainty and chaos. Given the world at the end of the 20th century, that uncertainty wasn't far away.

Friends and I visited the mansion in San Jose that was built by Sarah Winchester, the heir to the Winchester gun fortune. The story told to me was that she was in the midst of building an incredible mansion when the San Francisco earthquake hit in 1906. She was trapped in her bedroom for a long period of time with no way to utilize either the doors or windows in that room. In the aftermath, she responded to the earthquake by building doors to nowhere, stairs that stopped, and secret passages. Images from that visit never left my mind.

When I joined the USC faculty in Washington, I decided it was time to buy a real house. I found an older house in Washington that clearly needed renovation. Before I moved into the house I tore down a wall in the dining room. Soon after I did a major modification on the kitchen. Then I expanded the living room to include the space from the front porch. Then I built a room over the garage. And finally I expanded one of the bedrooms on the second floor and cantilevered it to become a spacious study. My friends who had joined me on the Winchester Mystery Tour started to call me Mrs. Winchester since I didn't seem to be able to stop building. I argued that it was easier to change my existing house than to move. Regardless. I have always had the urge to find ways make changes and stir things up.

It's clear when one takes a look at my CV that it is hard to characterize my career. By using the term "pracademic" I have described myself as someone who operates in both the world of practice and the academic world. I have found myself comfortable in both worlds. While they are different (with quite different expectations and reward systems), those differences are not always acknowledged as a part of reality. Indeed, fields such as public administration and public policy cannot survive without finding ways to bring the insights of both cultures together. I have argued that both approaches were present in the development of the policy and management fields but are less visible and available today. There are limited opportunities for faculty members to move between the academia to the world of practitioners. As a result, I have been involved in creating the Pracademic Fellowship inside of the American Political Science Association. It is an opportunity for faculty members to recreate the historical experience of joining theory and practice by spending time working closely with an official in an agency or organization and bring that reality to their classrooms.

Over the years I have found a way to create or respond to chaos, complexity and uncertainty and to imprint my own perspectives on my dwelling, my work environment, and other aspects of my life. Clearly, my television-watching patterns represent that urge. It has been important for me to move through the years avoiding labels and categories. I have noted that sometimes I felt as if I was in the wrong generation – my behavior either is a remnant of an earlier generation or is predictive of a future generation. Sometimes this has been successful, other times it has not. But it has led to an interesting collection of experiences.

A NETWORK AS A FAMILY

Perhaps the most positive result of my peripatetic career over the years has been the development of a group of very good friends drawn from different settings and experiences. Modern technology (especially Skype) has allowed me to keep in touch (both visually and substantively) with a wide range of friends across the globe. It's not unusual for me to chat with friends in Hong Kong, Australia, Israel and India, often combining our professional interests with family accounts and other personal issues. This collection of people has turned into my extended family, joining my blood relatives as a support mechanism. While I have never lived in an environment that is structured like the shtetl in Eastern Europe where some of my family members were originally found, my extended family operates like a virtual community. It's always a great pleasure for me to be able to link seemingly disparate people together for whatever reason. These relationships are nourished through personal relationships as well as relationships that are linked to professional meetings and joint research efforts.

This set of relationships has moved beyond my generation. Since I do not have children of my own, I have developed close relationships with children of my friends and family. As the son of one of my first cousins once noted, he felt that in many ways I behaved as an aunt, not as a cousin to him. In another case, the son of a close friend found it easy to use me as a surrogate for his parents after their deaths. I have taken great pleasure in the way that I am able to communicate with the younger generation through teaching and mentoring.

WHAT DOES IT MEAN TO AGE?

Because both of our parents died relatively early (especially my father who died at forty-nine) my brother Arthur and I both had the assumption that we too would not live to what has come to be defined as old age (a standard that as a result of scientific and demographic changes continues to move upward). While my brother retired from his teaching job when he turned sixty-five, I have avoided moving to a completely retired state. I have focused on the negative example of my grandfather who was required to retire as the head of the St. Paul Talmud Torah. Within months – having lost his work focus – he exhibited symptoms of severe dementia. That experience was something I sought to avoid. As a result, my last three jobs to this point were variations on a quasi-retired theme. I continue to teach (usually at a reduced load), to publish as an academic, and to be involved in a variety of professional activities that increasingly are found across the globe. Generally I have found that my energy level continues and I always enjoy it when acquaintances are surprised that I have turned eighty. Even my doctor characterized my overall age-related condition as closer to seventy than eighty. And many of my close friends who are retired find it strange that I do continue to be professionally active.

At the same time, it is clear that I am mortal. I do find that my energy level is not what it once was, even a few years ago. During this period I have discovered a range of health problems that I would have ignored in earlier years. As one friend said to me recently, "It's a good thing I am retired because I don't know how I would have time to go to all of my doctors' appointments if I were still working full time."

I don't know if anyone has studied the subjects of conversations between friends who are over seventy-five; I would bet that the subject of those conversations is overwhelmingly focused on health and medical issues. A friend reported that one of her friends called that conversation "an organ recital." It's hard to focus on the state of the world when your foot is painful and your mobility is limited.

There are clearly other things that have changed for me that are probably related to aging. I think twice about purchasing something for my house and haven't continued my past renovation efforts in my present dwelling. I turn down requests for involvement in some professional activities. While I have always been known as an outspoken person, I am probably clearer (and blunter) about my views. And I do try to spend time with younger people and serve as a mentor to them. I get great pleasure of seeing how my nieces have moved along their professional tracks and are finding ways to work out their own careers.

Some of my ambivalence toward aging stems from the limited examples of this natural process that have been provided by my extended family. There were few members of the family who lived to eighty. And most of those who approached that age spent years in a facility with a very limited quality of life. That is something I want to avoid. Still, for me, aging is a category that is quite different than others. And it's hard to ignore it. It's clear to me that aging gracefully is a difficult art form.

IGNORING CATEGORIES

As I reflect on my life it seems to me that I have had opportunities that were created by the changes that took place in the economic and social conditions in the U.S. I was a first generation American whose experiences growing up in South Dakota allowed me to maintain the values of generations of family members in Jewish communities both in Europe and the U.S. and yet, at the same time, draw from the environment of a small Midwestern American city. The flux that was found in the U.S. in the World War II and post War years opened doors of possibilities in education and work for me that eventually created opportunities to be a part of the social and political changes in the 1960s. My personal idiosyncrasies allowed me to move out of a predictable career path and to try new things and explore other settings.

I believe that these elements of constant change and flux provided opportunities for me that were not predictable. But those opportunities are not really common today. This current generation has many opportunities in work and lifestyle but its members do not live in an economic environment that allows them to take the kind of risks that

I was able to take. Despite this, perhaps this generation can find a way to identify elements of change, complexity and flux that provide them with the ability to try new things and explore other settings.

CONCLUSIONS

I began this memoir by emphasizing three themes that serve as an organizing principle for the pages that followed. I return to them in this concluding chapter.

Theme One argues that people change but usually maintain attributes of their earlier life. My story began in Aberdeen, South Dakota, and drew on those experiences that are rooted in my family, the community and in Judaism. Despite my wanderings over the years, I hold on to many of those experiences. These are represented by articles in my home, my values, and my indirect pathway to an academic career.

I described Theme Two as a belief that few of us can be described in simple and clear categories. Most of us contain contradictions and conflicts as we move through the world. My story illustrated several of those contradictions. They include the conflict between change and tradition (especially dealing with Judaism), operating inside or outside the "system", drawing on skills as an analyst or as an advocate, and working as a practitioner or an academic.

Theme Three acknowledges that change comes in unexpected ways, often as a result of unanticipated experiences. Most of us live in the midst of a fairly chaotic world and try to be open to new possibilities that may change the direction of earlier plans. Perhaps the most dramatic example of this was found in my discovery of the box of letters and materials that gave me a very different view of my mother than the one I had developed throughout the years. Travel and responding to changes in the political and social environment are other examples of unanticipated experiences.

This volume indicates that it has been difficult for me to locate myself in simple categories. I have always lived in multiple worlds and have tried to juggle the constraints and possibilities in all of them. That sometimes creates conflict and confusion. But it has led to an interesting life.

Americanization Class, Milwaukee, Wisconsin, Norman Radin 3rd from right, back row, circa 1918

Edelman Family, St. Paul, Minnesota. Sophie Edelman in middle of back row, 1920s

Sophie Edelman, circa 1934

Norman Radin, circa 1936

Sophie, Beryl, and Norman Radin, circa 1937

Beryl Radin at Victory Garden Parade, World War II, circa 1943

Beryl, Sophie, and Arthur Radin, circa 1945

Beryl, Sophie, and Arthur Radin, circa 1950

March on Washington, August 1963. Beryl Radin at far right lower edge

Beryl and Sophie Radin, circa 1970

Cochin, India, circa 1992

Synagogue, Cochin, India, circa 1992

Arthur and Beryl Radin at Niece Anneke's wedding

Jewish Cemetery at Quba, Azerbaijan, circa 2003

Rugs in Synagogue at Quba, Azerbaijan, circa 2003

Synagogue at Quba, Azerbaijan, circa 2003

Picture of Synagogue in Aberdeen, South Dakota, on line 2016

CHRONOLOGY

1904: Sophie Edelman, age 4, arrives in the U.S. with her parents and brother. They move to St. Paul, Minnesota.

1908: Norman Radin, age 12, arrives in the U.S. with his parents, brother and sisters. They move to Milwaukee, Wisconsin.

1918: Sophie Edelman graduates from high school.

Circa 1920: Sophie Edelman moves to New York City to work in the office of an Oriental rug company.

Circa 1932: Sophie Edelman returns to St. Paul. Norman Radin joins the staff of Investors Syndicate in Minneapolis, Minnesota.

1934: Sophie Edelman and Norman Radin meet at a party, become engaged, and marry in August. They move to Aberdeen, South Dakota.

1936: Beryl Radin is born in Aberdeen.

1938: Arthur Radin is born in Aberdeen.

1942 to 1954: Beryl Radin attends public school in Aberdeen. Lives through World War II.

1946: Norman Radin dies of a heart attack in Madison, Wisconsin.

1954: Beryl graduates from high school, applies and is accepted to Antioch College in Yellow Springs, Ohio

1954 to 1958: Beryl attends Antioch College, has Antioch work experiences in Washington, D.C., Yellow Springs, Ohio, and New York City.

1958: Beryl graduates from Antioch, majors in history. Decides to go to graduate school at the University of Minnesota for American Studies.

1958 to 1960: Beryl completes course work for a master's degree in American Studies.

1960: Beryl moves to Philadelphia, Pennsylvania, has several jobs, including one at the Amalgamated Clothing Workers Union and a local political campaign. Active in the Philadelphia branch of the Congress of Racial Equality (CORE).

1963: Beryl attends the March on Washington.

November 1963 to August 1965: Beryl moves to Washington, D.C. to work at the U.S. Commission on Civil Rights as the Assistant Information Officer.

September 1965 to August 1966: Beryl lives in London, active in immigrant rights organizations, travels throughout Europe.

September 1966 to July 1969: Beryl returns to Washington, D.C., works as a consultant for various civil rights and union groups. Decides to pursue a PhD at the University of California at Berkeley.

August 1969 to August 1971: Beryl moves to Berkeley, California to begin PhD program in Social Policies Planning.

September 1971 to August 1973: Beryl returns to Washington, D.C., finishes dissertation and teaches at Goucher College outside of Baltimore.

March 1972: Sophie Radin dies in St. Paul, Minnesota.

September 1973 to August 1977: Beryl joins the faculty of the LBJ School of Public Affairs at the University of Texas at Austin, teaching master's level graduate students.

September 1977 to August 1978: Beryl returns to Washington, D.C. Has a one-year assignment in both the Office of the Assistant Secretary for Planning and Evaluation, U.S. Department of Health, Education and Welfare and the President's Reorganization Project in the Office of Management and Budget.

September 1978 to March 1994: Beryl stays in Washington, D.C. to join the faculty of the University of Southern California's Washington Public Affairs Center. Chairs the DPA program, serves as director of the Center, has sabbatical assignment in Australia. Active in various professional organizations.

Summer 1990: Beryl has a Senior Fulbright fellowship in India at the Indian Institute of Public Administration.

April 1994 to August 1996: Beryl begins as professor and chair of the Department of Public Administration and Policy in the School of Public Affairs, Rockefeller College, SUNY, Albany, New York. Steps down as chair.

September 1996 to August 1998: Beryl returns to Washington and serves as a consultant in the Office of the Assistant Secretary for Management and Budget, Department of Health and Human Services. Continues as a one day a week consultant from 1998 to 2000.

September 1998 to January 2002: Beryl returns to Albany as Professor of Public Administration and Policy in the School of Public Affairs. Commutes between Washington and Albany during this period.

2000 to 2005: Beryl becomes managing editor of the Journal of Public Administration Research and Theory.

2000 to 2015: Visiting faculty in Australia, Denmark, Hong Kong, Azerbaijan, Israel.

January 2002 to August 2005: Beryl joins the faculty as Professor of Government and Public Administration in the School of Public Affairs, the University of Baltimore.

September 2005 to December 2011: Beryl returns to Washington and joins the faculty as a Scholar in Residence in the Department of Public Administration of the School of Public Affairs at American University.

January 2012 to the present: Beryl joins the faculty of the McCourt School of Public Policy at Georgetown University as an adjunct professor.

ABOUT THE AUTHOR

Beryl A. Radin is a semi-retired member of the faculty of the McCourt School of Public Policy at Georgetown University who continues to write and teach. She is someone who calls herself a "pracademic" – a person who spans the academic world and the world of a public policy practitioner. Her work has dealt with a range of public management and public policy issues. She is the author and coauthor of more than a dozen books, but this is her first memoir. Further information is available online at berylaradin.com.